All sorts of players from a variety of teams — but they all know how to celebrate a goal!

IAN OLNEY (ASTON VILLA)

IAN WRIGHT (CRYSTAL PALACE)

ANDY HINCHCLIFFE (left) and STEVE REDMOND lead the way for their Manchester City teammates.

PRICE £3.50

contents

The Topical Times FOOTBALL BOOK

Losing the FA Cup Final replay last season to Manchester United was a terrible disappointment. Especially since we had come so close to winning the first game. But at least I already had a winner's medal from my Wimbledon days — unlike the rest of my team-mates. I felt more sorry for them than for myself.

We came in for a lot of stick from the media for our style at Wembley, particularly in the replay. It was unjustified. Palace wanted to win the FA Cup. A man-for-man marking game seemed the best way against a team like Manchester United.

For much of the replay we succeeded. Our goalkeeper Nigel Martyn had far less to do than Les Sealey.

We weren't going to outplay anyone with sheer footballing skill. But we could frustrate them with our hard work and organisation.

That style overcame Liverpool in the semi-final, and I thought we could beat United the same way. We came so close — within seven minutes of winning the first game — but in the end it wasn't to be.

I've been a fan of greyhound racing. And that taught me from an early age that there are no certainties in sport.

If everything went according to form, and the favourite won every time, there would be no bookmakers. But you don't see many poor bookies around.

It's the same with football. Previous form never really matters much. It's what happens on the day that counts. I felt we could beat Liverpool at Villa Park — but I certainly didn't expect it to be anything like 4-3. That was unbelievable.

That result gave us the confidence to get the points that kept us in the First Division. Staying up was vital for me. The previous year I had been relegated with Newcastle United, and the last thing I wanted was to go back down again. I had had enough of fighting relegation with Newcastle.

If United had stayed up that year, I'd probably still be on Tyneside. I enjoyed my year there, even if results didn't go well.

I wasn't looking to get away,

race, and taking them for a walk. It helps me to forget about the pressures of football.

A previous dog I owned won eight races, and ran in an open event at Wembley Stadium. That was almost as big a thrill as playing there myself!

At one time I didn't think I was going to make the final against United. I badly damaged an ankle against Arsenal in April, and thought it would put me out for months.

My first thought was that it was broken. But it turned out to be damaged ligaments, and it was a race against time to get fit.

For a couple of weeks I spent more time in the treatment room than at home. But it paid off. I missed only three League games, and I was back in time to help us clinch our First Division place — with a win at Wimbledon.

Now I hope we can build on our Wembley experience this season. We've proved we have the potential for success at Selhurst Park.

GO OUT TO WIN!

That's the aim of Crystal Palace's ANDY THORN

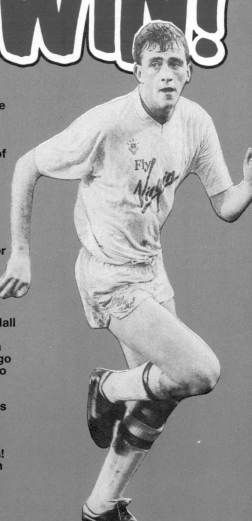

My type of game suits that approach. My job is to win the ball. I go out to win, not to please people. Of course, if you can win with style, that's great. But it's a bonus.

It was a blow to lose out with the Cup Final, but at least I made sure I took in the atmosphere of the occasion. The day just went by in a blur when I was there with Wimbledon.

With Palace I was more relaxed, able to savour the build-up and enjoy the day. Even though we lost it in the end, it was still a great season for Palace.

Staying in the First Division was the priority for us throughout the campaign. We took the cup matches as a break from struggling for League points, and that probably helped us get to Wembley.

Nobody will ever forget our semi-final victory over Liverpool. That was a fantastic match. Very few people gave us any chance beforehand, but I always had a sneaking feeling we would win.

Ever since I was a youngster

even after dropping back into the Second Division, but the club needed the money from my transfer.

Palace gave me the chance of First Division football again, and also the opportunity to get back to London, so I was happy to sign.

But I wouldn't have joined if I hadn't thought the club had the potential to challenge for honours, rather than just fight for survival at top level. I'm an ambitious player. I want to win things.

Away from the game, my main relaxation is my dogs. I own two greyhounds, Tonaroy Hall and Super Badger. I like nothing better than taking them out for a walk on my days off. Normally I go out on a Sunday with the dogs, to loosen up after a match.

I don't play any part in their training. That's left to the experts — like football training. I don't expect my dog trainer to tell me how to play football — so I don't tell him how to train greyhounds!

My enjoyment is seeing them

WORLD CUP SPECIAL

ITALIA '90

— WHEN THE PENALTY KICK WAS KING.

The World Cup is billed as football's most important tournament. Every four years each competition produces its own moments of drama and controversy — and Italia '90 was no exception.

Remember the exciting Cameroons and super sub Roger Milla?

Remember, too, the deadly goal-scoring of Schillaci, the skills of Lacatus, Stojkovic, Hagi, Giannini, Scifo, Dunga?

But the competition also brought its disappointments for players and countries. Highly-fancied Sweden, who topped their qualifying group, went home with three defeats against their name. European Championship runners-up Russia finished bottom of their group. Brazil made an early exit unable to capture the rhythm of previous years.

But perhaps the biggest disappointment of all was felt by hosts Italy.

They'd had high expectations of winning the tournament — and it was a bitter moment for them when they lost that penalty shoot-out to Argentina in the semi-finals.

Players, too, found luck against them.

Argentine goalkeeper Pumpido, whose blunder gave the Cameroons victory in the opening game, broke his leg in the second game. Bitter disappointment, too, for Argentina captain Maradona, as his team went down to an inglorious defeat in the final.

But perhaps the most lingering memory of Italia '90 will be the heart-stopping drama of the penalty shoot-out. For the spectators it brought added excitement. But for those who came out on the losing side it brought only despair.

The experts argued loud and long about the fairness of the shoot-out. Certainly there were occasions where the team that had been on the receiving end during normal play came out on top in the penalty decider. Perhaps the best examples of that were Argentina's triumphs over Yugoslavia and Italy.

Even in the games which didn't go to a shoot-out, penalties still proved crucial. England's game against the Cameroons had three, with Gary Lineker scoring twice from the spot.

Germany's winners against Czechoslovakia in the quarter-final and against Argentina in the final came from penalties.

But in the end, despite all the talk of luck, the team that won was the most consistent side in the competition. For that alone West Germany deserved to lift the World Cup.

For England, Scotland and the Republic of Ireland the tournament had its moments to look back on — and moments to forget.

The following pages look back at their bid for glory in Italia '90.

Anguish for Argentina's Maradona — joy for Germany's Matthäus and Voller.

SO NEAR —

THAT SUMS UP ENGLAND'S BID FOR GLORY IN ITALIA'90

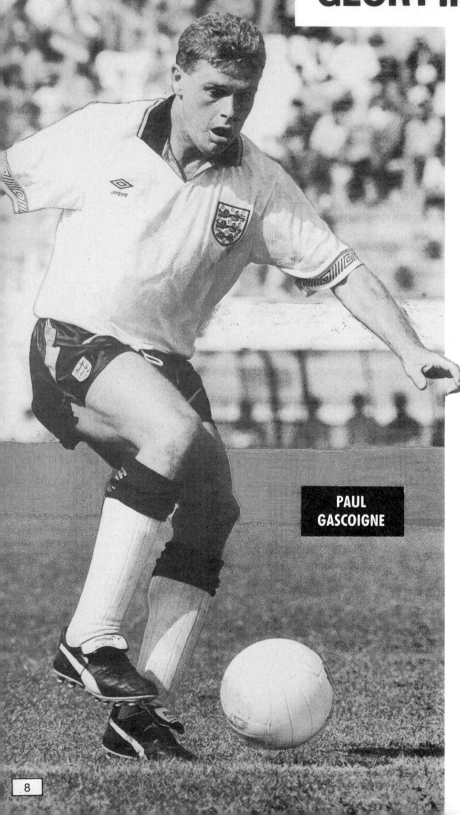

PAUL GASCOIGNE

So near — and yet so far. That's the story of England's World Cup.

So near to defeat first by Belgium, and then by Cameroon in the quarter-finals. So near to victory in the semi-final against Germany.

In the end they went so far — but not quite all the way. Their first World Cup Final appearance in 24 years was tantalisingly out of reach.

But it was a memorable experience for the England players. Several youngsters came through the World Cup to establish themselves as future international stars.

David Platt was one. The Aston Villa midfield player took over the role from injured skipper Bryan Robson, and looked every inch the part.

Handed the awesome responsibility of taking the third penalty in the semi-final shoot-out, he scored confidently from the spot.

"I was a bit nervous thinking about it. But on my way to the kick, I passed German captain Lothar Matthäus coming back from taking his penalty," reveals David.

"He gave me a wink, and a pat on the back, which was a really nice gesture, and completely settled me down. That was a sign of the spirit in which the match was played.

"It was very disappointing to lose the game on penalties, but you go into a game, and if you don't win it after two hours you go into a penalty shoot-out. You know that beforehand, and you have to accept it."

One of the greatest memories the players will retain from Italy, is of the way the West Germans delayed their own victory celebrations after the semi-final to commiserate with the England players.

Matthäus, the German skipper, put his arm round Chris Waddle in a genuine gesture of sympathy after the Marseille star had put his penalty 'way over the bar. The other German players showed similar respect.

YET SO FAR!

Gary Lineker displayed the same attitude after the third-place play-off match against Italy. Despite defeat in controversial circumstances, Gary made a point of congratulating 'Toto' Schillaci, the Italian striker who had taken over from him as the World Cup 'Golden Boot' winner for top scorer.

England came so close. For the second World Cup in succession, they lost to the eventual winners, and played well enough to have won.

But they came away with so much credit, and a genuine optimism for the future. David Platt sums it up.

"It was a great experience to be on the same pitch as players like Gullit, Van Basten, Matthäus, Giannini, Schillaci and the rest," says David. "I feel it can only make me a better player.

"I hope that Aston Villa as well as England will get the benefits in the next few years.

"I went out to Italy just happy to be one of the 22. I had my fingers crossed up to the last minute that I would be selected. I never expected to play such a part.

"I enjoyed scoring all my three goals, but the volley against Belgium was my favourite. That was a bit special.

"But I don't see myself as just a goalscorer, either for England, or Villa. I feel I am a midfield player, with defensive responsibilities. I don't have a licence just to attack.

"I hope people don't expect me to go on scoring goals like that. If this season I don't get so many goals, I won't worry. The manager is the only one I have to please."

The players have their own off-the-field memories of the World Cup, some centred on the pre-tournament golfing competition, arranged for the squad at their hotel in Cagliari.

Liverpool's Steve McMahon won the cup in a play-off on the first extra hole, and was almost as proud as if he'd won the Masters! The trophy was carefully carried around Italy, and back home to Liverpool.

"They'll not get it back from me," said Steve. "I'll treasure that cup, I had to work hard to win it."

John Barnes created a stir on the golfing day. He'd never played before and took no part in the main tournament.

But after an hour or two with the professional on the driving range, John took part in the 'long driving' event — and powered his first drive over 300 yards down the middle!

The club promised to erect a special plaque to commemorate the feat, and Barnes took the prize for the longest drive.

There were other little moments. Gary Lineker was shocked to discover he had lost a stone in weight during the match against Cameroon — he hasn't really got any spare pounds to lose.

GARY LINEKER

But he was relieved to learn that the scales in the dressing room were faulty — he'd only lost seven pounds, about normal for a match in that heat.

The players, who were weighed before and after every match, to check for dehydration, were under instruction to replace lost fluids with special isotonic drinks.

The careful medical and training preparations paid off. England were able to play three matches in succession involving extra time — the equivalent of playing one full extra match — without distress.

Paul Gascoigne surprised even himself the way he could keep going for two hours. When manager Bobby Robson found him playing tennis in 90 degree heat, the day after the match, he came to the conclusion that Gazza is hyperactive.

"He can't sit still for a minute, he needs a 24-hour guard on him," said Robson.

And after that he made sure Gascoigne had the hotel room next to his own, so that he could keep an eye on England's biggest asset.

Most of the England players believe the World Cup experience has improved their game. None more so than Wolves' striker, Steve Bull.

Bully found the World Cup footballs hard to handle at first.

"I called them balloons," confesses Steve. "They were so light and bouncy, you could knock 60-70 yard balls with them.

"If you could control one of them, you could control anything. Coming back into English football was like playing with a bag of cement.

"Mind you, the best players in the world could control the ball all right. Some of the goals scored were different class. It would be nice to think I could score goals like that.

"I'm going to work at developing the sort of skills I saw out there. The World Cup was a new experience for me, and I loved it.

"I spent a lot of time on the bench, which was frustrating, but it was great just to be one of the best 22 players in the country.

"It might be a once-in-a-lifetime experience for me, but I hope not. I will be 29 next time round, and I want to be in the team for that tournament."

Every player in the squad would love to be there again. But some know they won't. Peter Shilton retired from international football after the final match in Italy, and Bryan Robson and Terry Butcher will almost certainly not be around for the 1994 event.

The future is in the hands of players like Paul Gascoigne, Paul Parker, Mark Wright, Des Walker and David Platt.

They came of age in Italy, and won bronze medals for fourth place.

Can they make it gold in the USA?

JACK'S LADS!

They did the Republic of Ireland proud!

Goalkeeping hero PAT BONNER greets victory over Romania.

DUBLIN'S O'Connell Street is like most roads in a big city. It's almost always packed with cars and pedestrians. Yet on five occasions this summer it was strangely quiet. The reason? Like thousands of people elsewhere in the Republic of Ireland, the folk in Dublin were tuned in to their television sets, watching Jack Charlton's side battle it out in the World Cup Finals.

And it was an equally enthusiastic support that had travelled to Italy to see their heroes in action.

An estimated 20,000 Irish fans followed their team across Italy — making friends wherever they went. It was reckoned that apart from West Germany and Italy, the Republic of Ireland were the best supported team in the competition.

And while the football experts may not have been overjoyed about the no-nonsense, no-frills style of the Republic, the fans were behind their team all the way.

And certainly the players deserved much of the praise that their fans lavished on them. They weren't expected even to qualify for the World Cup Finals — but they did!

Then they weren't expected to progress beyond their qualifying group — but they did!

Then the Republic were given no chance of beating highly-fancied Romania — but they did!

Their dramatic, penalty shoot-out win over Romania put them into the quarter-finals against hot favourites Italy.

This time there was no happy ending. Italy won — but by the narrowest of margins.

The 1990 World Cup was over for the Republic of Ireland — but their fans will never forget the efforts of Jack's Lads.

Team boss **JACK CHARLTON** and right-hand man **MAURICE SETTERS** watch the action.

...eld dynamo **RAY HOUGHTON** ...n typical non-stop action.

Defensive duo **MICK McCARTHY** and **KEVIN MORAN** (right) team up to celebrate.

DON'T CALL US

SCOTLAND did not progress to the second stage of the World Cup Finals, but there's no way I will accept we failed in Italy.

We had been written off by so many people even before we boarded the plane for the world's biggest football tournament. What seemed to be forgotten was that just winning a place in the Finals was a remarkable achievement in itself.

Consider the teams in our qualifying group. Yugoslavia proved in Italy what a class side they are and underlined why they were the first country to book their place in the Finals.

We were actually only third favourites to qualify, with France considered by most people to have a better chance of getting through from the group. And, at one point, even Norway were suggested as possible runners-up to Yugoslavia.

Nevertheless, because we have an excellent record in qualifying in past World Cups, the Scottish fans take it for granted we will get there, which puts a lot of pressure on the squad.

Perhaps pressure is the wrong word. I preferred to regard it as a challenge to follow in the footsteps of Scotland's previous World Cup squads. And, if you want to get anywhere in the game, these are the sort of challenges you must face.

We showed a lot of character to reach our fifth Finals in a row, and there were a lot of very good French players sitting at home watching the tournament wishing they were in our place.

We arrived in Italy knowing the draw had given us difficult opponents in our opening group. Brazil are always a force in the World Cup Finals, and Sweden had topped their qualifying group, which included England, without losing a game. They were respected throughout Europe as a well-organised side.

The fourth country in Group C, Costa Rica, were virtually unknown at this level, and we were unfortunate to be drawn against them in our opening match.

The Luigi Ferraris Stadium in Genoa, where our first two games were staged, was a magnificent setting, and our supporters were right behind us.

We were all confident going into the game against the Central Americans, but we always realised it was going to be a difficult match.

Unfortunately, despite all our chances, we didn't score to give

MO JOHNSTON

our tremendous support the victory they wanted so badly. And when the Costa Ricans raced away to hit the only goal of the game, we found ourselves on the wrong end of a freak result.

Once again, the character within the squad was shown as we bounced right back, and by the time the Sweden game came around five days later, we were determined to get right back into the reckoning for a place in round two.

Of course, the Swedes, having lost their opening match against Brazil, were every bit as desperate for the points. And that's why our victory over them, and the manner in which it was achieved, proved such a boost to our morale.

We'd never thought we were down and out. With two points in the bag going into the last match against Brazil, we felt confident we could get through to the next round.

One point against Brazil would have been enough to see us through to the second stage for the first time in Scotland's World Cup history, and we came within nine minutes of achieving this.

That's how much of the game was left when they scored, and, despite all our efforts, we couldn't get the equaliser. It was just one of those nights when the ball wouldn't go in for us. I had a very good chance before they scored, but, even though my header beat 'keeper Taffarel, Brazil captain Branco was on the line to boot it clear.

That was actually the second time I thought I was going to open my World Cup account. Earlier, against Sweden, I had a shot saved by 'keeper Ravelli's foot, then, as I raced after the rebound, was brought down to earn the penalty which Maurice Johnston converted to put us 2-0 up.

Unlike the atmosphere after the Sweden game, however, the mood in the dressing-room following our defeat by Brazil was understandably deflated.

Back in our hotel, we all had a meal, then sat around discussing the match and trying to work out what results were required from the remaining group matches if we were to get through with two points.

Unfortunately, those results didn't run our way, though I don't think any of us were surprised as lucky breaks seemed to give us a wide berth throughout our stay in Italy.

This was best illustrated the day after our final match when we watched Uruguay struggle against South Korea. At the end of 90

FAILURES!

minutes, the game was still goalless, which meant we would go into a draw with Austria later that evening to see who progressed to the last 16.

But, two minutes into injury time, the South Americans scored, and that door was slammed in our faces.

In our hotel we watched all the drama unfolding, not knowing if we were packing to move on to another venue — or home!

Later that night, we sat in our rooms watching the final two first-round games involving Egypt against England, and Eire against Holland. We needed two 1-0 wins to give us a last chance of qualifying but the Dutch and Irish drew, and we were out.

I suppose this didn't really come as any great surprise because we'd taken so many kicks in the teeth in the preceeding ten days that we all knew deep down the permutation of results we needed was not going to materialise.

I still think considering how we played over the three games, we deserved to reach the second round. Okay, in the first game, against Costa Rica, we didn't perform as well as we could, and we should have scored and won. But we did create enough chances to get both points, certainly more than either Brazil or Sweden did against them.

And I rate our performance against Sweden as probably the best Scotland have ever produced in the World Cup Finals.

That left just the Brazil match in which I thought we played well against quality players. As I said, unfortunately it was just one of those nights.

We were able to go home with our heads held high, and it was nice to be met by cheering fans when we arrived back at Glasgow Airport. We gave our all and regained our pride. No one could ask for more than that.

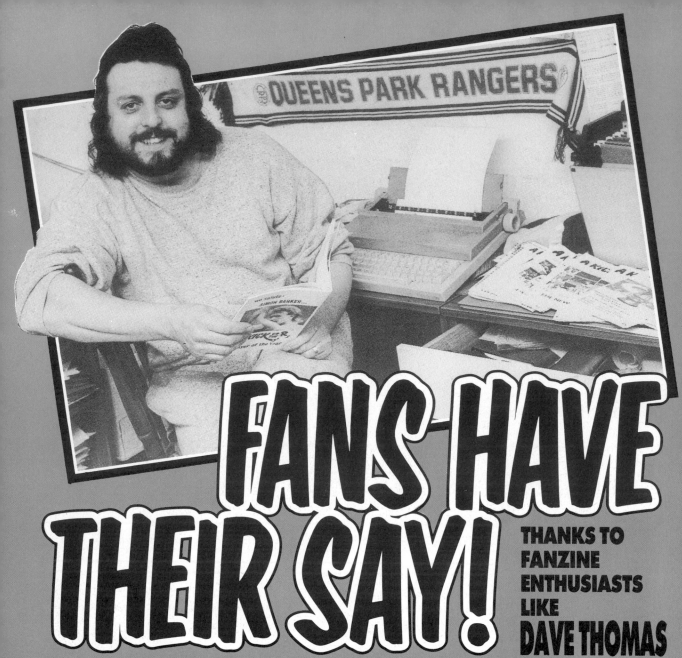

FANS HAVE THEIR SAY!

THANKS TO FANZINE ENTHUSIASTS LIKE DAVE THOMAS

There are now more than 300 of them, acting as the voice of football fans all over the country. What are they? "Fanzines" of course.

Fan magazines, to give them their full title, have sprouted up over the past couple of years or so. Kitchen tables countrywide have found themselves covered with clippings, cuttings and paste as deadlines near for the home-made publications.

"A Kick Up The R's", one such publication, is put together single-handedly by Queen's Park Rangers' fan Dave Thomas in his home near Whitchurch in Shropshire. It was one of the first on the market and now frequently sells all of its 2000 print.

But for all its success, putting it together is still a very hard slog. Dave takes up the story.

"I got the idea for the magazine in 1987. That February we heard that QPR, the team I have supported for 24 years, were to merge with neighbours Fulham.

"Obviously the supporters of both clubs didn't like the idea. I realised there was no "voice" for the fans. That summer I started the magazine.

"It wasn't intended to be a protest publication. It was put together as an outlet for the fans views on anything to do with QPR. Since that first issue, which sold 1500 copies, the magazine hasn't looked back.

"Once the fans had seen the magazine they responded very well. People submitted articles and letters, too. My first issue was 24 pages, by the seventh it was up to 68 pages.

"People seem to think fanzines are out to criticise clubs. That isn't wholly true, and certainly not right in my case. They're an alternative, to the match programme".

But the fanzine doesn't put itself together. Dave has a lot of work to do to get every edition out. In fact, he estimates producing each edition takes 200 hours of his time.

"I put the magazine out every two months. The whole production process takes up to six weeks, and I also have all my letters to answer.

"Each issue generates about 90-100 letters. It can take two weeks to catch up on that alone.

"While I do all the production, there are other people who contribute.

"When I know a deadline date I inform people whom I have had material from before. I write to them hoping for an article. That gives the magazine different opinions and viewpoints.

"When I get articles back, I type them all out again. I have my own electronic typewriter which is a real help and, sometimes I borrow a word processor and its operator.

"If I had a word processor of my own it would cut down 70 per cent of my workload.

"Then changes have to be made to the typed-out articles. When this happens I type the corrections on to another piece of paper, cut them up and stick them on to the story I originally typed up.

"When all the corrections and changes have been made I have a full page made up in the way you do a jigsaw. For this process you need a craft knife and steel rule to cut out and move sections, then all the pieces are stuck to the page.

"This has to be done for every page, then the headings and titles are added by affixing large 'letraset' letters. Every page is made up this way.

"When the full page is completed it is then photocopied at my local shop. That goes for all 68 pages.

"When all the pages have been copied, I put them together to form the finished magazine. That is then the master copy.

"All this sounds straight forward but, like every other publication, I have to run to deadlines. To make these I often spend the final 48 hours working almost non-stop. I sleep downstairs in an armchair with a blanket. I grab a couple of hours kip wherever I can and then it's back down to work.

"It gets so hectic because last minute changes are needed to make sure the magazine is as up-to-date as possible.

"The master copy then has to go to the printers in Sheffield. But I

don't trust the post. After all, if it was lost, all my work would be wasted and there would be no magazine for another two months.

"So I drive to Sheffield and drop the master copy in at the printers myself. There, 2000 copies are run off all on re-cycled paper. We are doing our bit for the environment too!

"When the finished article is ready it's down to Loftus Road to sell it. I make a 400 mile round trip from Shropshire to London with all the magazines.

"I park as near to the ground as possible, often arriving at 10 o'clock in the morning. Four friends help me to sell copies outside the ground. Without their help it would be impossible to distribute the magazine."

But apart from match day sales, Dave also has 120 subscribers to cater for. These are the people who pay in advance for a year's issues and then receive each copy through the post when it's produced.

"Apart from having subscribers all over England, from as far afield as Cornwall and Tyne and Wear, I also send copies abroad," Dave explains.

"On my list are fans in Norway, Austria, West Germany, Sweden, the USA, Canada, Australia and New Zealand. They all want to keep up with happenings at our club.

"The magazine is really a labour of love for me, and it makes everything worthwhile when people stop just to say how much they enjoy it, or write to tell me to keep up the good work.

"As long as people keep buying the magazine I'll continue to put it all together.

"I print 2000 and often sell out, but I'm never left with any more than 200. Sales usually depend on Rangers' opposition at the time the magazine is on sale and also how well the team are doing. But to sell that amount at a club with an average gate around the 12,000 mark isn't bad," ends Dave.

MEL STERLAND *Leeds United*

RICHARD GOUGH
Rangers

17

FOOTBALL'S A GREAT LIFE!

OVER the last ten years, it's been my privilege to have played in some of the most famous 'derby' matches in Europe. With Manchester United I played against Manchester City; in Italy I played for Milan against Internazionale; and in Glasgow for Rangers against Celtic.

All games played in a white-hot atmosphere in stadiums packed with passionate fans.

Those matches were great occasions, highlights of a wonderful career at club level. But I can honestly say I still get just as much enjoyment from a kick-around on the training ground.

It doesn't take a full house for me to get keyed up for a game of football. I don't even need three men and a dog to watch. Just give me a piece of ground and a football, and I'm away. I love every game I play, whether it's a League match, a Cup Final or a five-a-side training session.

Enthusiasm is more important than anything else, especially when you get older. If you lose your enthusiasm for the game, you're finished, however young you are.

I've had a long playing career, but I still feel great because I enjoy playing, and training.

I have always looked after myself physically, and if you do that I believe you can carry on as long as you want to.

Last year, when I left Glasgow Rangers to join Queen's Park Rangers, I decided it was time I began to take care with my diet. It wasn't a question of being overweight, I just felt I should be careful over what I ate.

The result was I lost nine pounds in weight, and I never felt better. I was really sharp, and that helped me to adjust to the pace of First Division football.

GOING to QPR presented me with a new challenge. I was introduced to the sweeper system for the first time in my career — despite my three years in Italy.

Most teams in Italy line up with a sweeper, but my club, Milan, were the only side in the League which played with a flat back four. Slotting into the QPR system was a new experience.

There's no doubt that with the right players, it can be very effective. We have Paul Parker doing the sweeper's job at Rangers. There's probably no player in England better equipped for the role.

He is very quick, physically and mentally, and reads the game so well. Paul is learning when to bring the ball out of defence himself, and how to make use of the space he gets. I believe he could do a great job in that role for England at international level.

When I came back into English football, a lot of people seemed to think that I was playing more positively than I used to. I don't go along with that.

I'm not doing anything different these days. I'm still aiming to keep the game simple. I'm trying to pass the ball to a player wearing the same colour of shirt as I am.

I've always remembered a remark that former England manager Ron Greenwood once made. That every time you pass the ball, whether it's a five-yard or fifty-yard pass, the game situation has changed. Even if you get the ball straight back, the angles have altered, the pattern has shifted.

I try to pass the ball to my own players, and not give it away unnecessarily. The best teams keep it simple, knock the ball around, and wait for things to happen.

Liverpool are the best example of a team that keeps the game simple. They just knock the ball around, and work hard, supporting the man on the ball, giving him plenty of options. They play with patience, waiting for openings to appear. I believe we can play like that at QPR. We certainly have the players with the skill to do it.

Anybody can kick the ball sixty yards up the field and give it away. Good players want the ball, they hate to give away possession.

It was great experience for me to play in Italy, where every player treats the ball with respect. They love to keep it. Possession is never wasted.

I really enjoyed my time at Milan. The football and the lifestyle were great. When my contract was up I decided to quit Italy altogether rather than join a different club just in case a change of club would alter my liking for Italy.

Even now my Sunday lunch is programmed around the satellite TV games from Italy. Football in Italy is a major event. It's the family day out. Everyone puts on their Sunday best to go to the match.

The approach is totally different to England. It would be great to make our football more of a family occasion, and encourage wives and children to go together.

I know that Trevor Francis was much influenced by his experiences in Italy, and tried to put his ideas into practice when he became manager of QPR. I can't say why he didn't succeed, but I did have a lot of sympathy for him.

In Italy there is much greater discipline among players. They have to be more committed towards their clubs. I'm not against that. I think there is much to be gained from the Italian attitude.

It was strange to negotiate my move to QPR with Trevor, and then find out he had left the club

SO SAYS QUEEN'S PARK RANGERS' RAY WILKINS

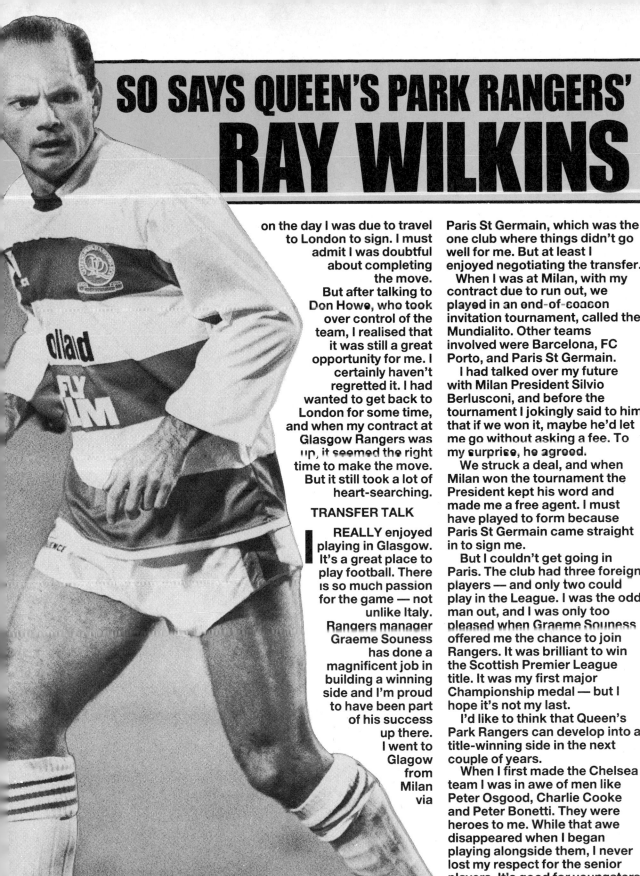

on the day I was due to travel to London to sign. I must admit I was doubtful about completing the move. But after talking to Don Howe, who took over control of the team, I realised that it was still a great opportunity for me. I certainly haven't regretted it. I had wanted to get back to London for some time, and when my contract at Glasgow Rangers was up, it seemed the right time to make the move. But it still took a lot of heart-searching.

TRANSFER TALK

I REALLY enjoyed playing in Glasgow. It's a great place to play football. There is so much passion for the game — not unlike Italy. Rangers manager Graeme Souness has done a magnificent job in building a winning side and I'm proud to have been part of his success up there. I went to Glagow from Milan via Paris St Germain, which was the one club where things didn't go well for me. But at least I enjoyed negotiating the transfer.

When I was at Milan, with my contract due to run out, we played in an end-of-season invitation tournament, called the Mundialito. Other teams involved were Barcelona, FC Porto, and Paris St Germain.

I had talked over my future with Milan President Silvio Berlusconi, and before the tournament I jokingly said to him that if we won it, maybe he'd let me go without asking a fee. To my surprise, he agreed.

We struck a deal, and when Milan won the tournament the President kept his word and made me a free agent. I must have played to form because Paris St Germain came straight in to sign me.

But I couldn't get going in Paris. The club had three foreign players — and only two could play in the League. I was the odd man out, and I was only too pleased when Graeme Souness offered me the chance to join Rangers. It was brilliant to win the Scottish Premier League title. It was my first major Championship medal — but I hope it's not my last.

I'd like to think that Queen's Park Rangers can develop into a title-winning side in the next couple of years.

When I first made the Chelsea team I was in awe of men like Peter Osgood, Charlie Cooke and Peter Bonetti. They were heroes to me. While that awe disappeared when I began playing alongside them, I never lost my respect for the senior players. It's good for youngsters to have players around they can look up to. I hope my enthusiasm and attitude provides a good example for the younger players at QPR. But whatever happens, I shall go on enjoying my football.

19

JOHN SHERIDAN
Sheffield Wednesday

NORMAN WHITESIDE
Everton

PASTA BUT NO PIZZAS!

THAT'S THE ADVICE FROM FITNESS EXPERT PROFESSOR TOMMY REILLY

EVERTON have called in an expert in nutrition to help their players cope with the rigours of modern day football.

They approached Professor Tom Reilly, who is head of 'Sport and Exercise Sciences' at Liverpool Polytechnic. He was only too pleased to give them the benefit of his scientific knowledge.

"Top class football is a much more energy-sapping game than it used to be," says Tom. "Years ago players stood still and watched other members of the team playing with the ball. If a player felt tired he could 'hide' and let the others carry him. Not any more! In fact, I compare the energy levels of players running 'off the ball' for 90 minutes these days to an athlete running in a competitive marathon.

"Fans go to a game and are convinced they see all the action. But really they have no idea of the amount of running put in by most players. Of course, the manager and coaches on the bench know what is going on but even they can accuse a lad of 'hiding' in the last 15 minutes, when he is plainly exhausted."

To counteract this exhaustion, the prof's advice is fairly simple.

"We have proved," he says, "that a high carbohydrate diet for two days prior to a game is beneficial. Pasta, cannelloni, spaghetti, etc. (but no pizzas). Also bread, rice, cereals, and boiled or jacket potatoes. No fat, milk, butter, cheese, fish or steaks should be taken, but plenty of fruit is good, especially bananas.

"This type of food provides muscle energy for long periods. After the game the players should have one more meal of the same carbohydrate foods, and then they can eat what they fancy until two days before the next match."

Tom has also given advice on jet-lag. On one occasion Everton arrived back at Liverpool Airport at 11.15 a.m. after a very long flight. Although exhausted and ready for bed, they were whisked off to the practice ground for a training session.

"It seems cruel, but they thanked me afterwards," said Tom.

Professor Reilly admits that his high energy diets cannot guarantee success.

"Luck comes into the game," he adds. "And after all, there is no substitute for skill."

PROFESSOR REILLY — in the laboratory with the "Fitness Analyser".

PAUL GASCOIGNE *Tottenham Hotspur*

PAUL ELLIOTT
Celtic

24

STEVE BOULD
Arsenal

STEVE SUTTON *Nottingham Forest*

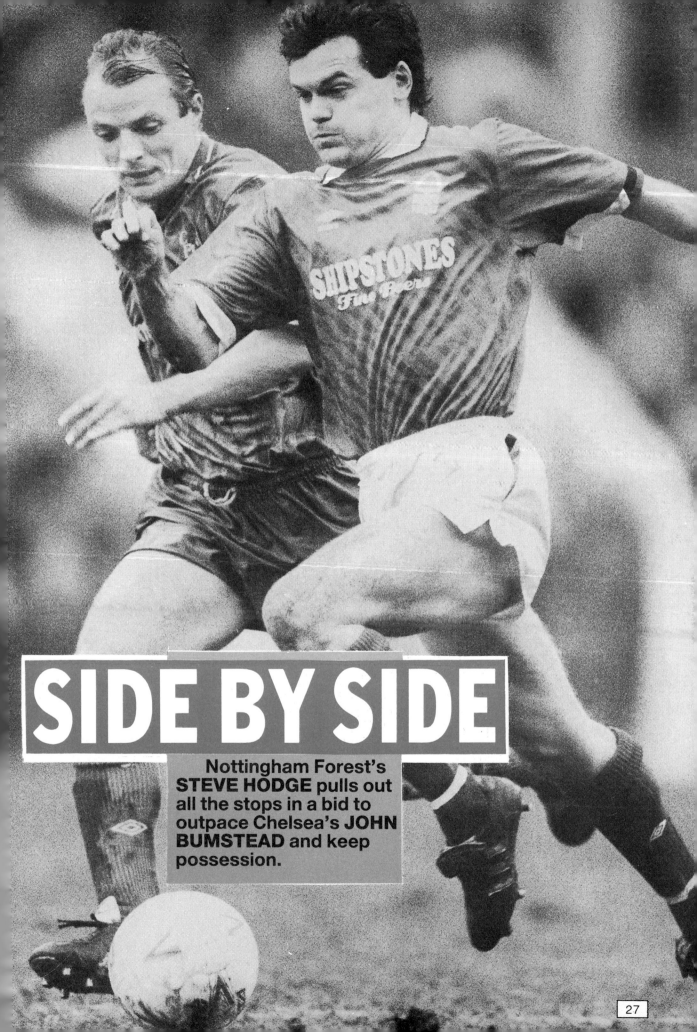

SIDE BY SIDE

Nottingham Forest's **STEVE HODGE** pulls out all the stops in a bid to outpace Chelsea's **JOHN BUMSTEAD** and keep possession.

27

BRUCE GROBBELAAR
Liverpool

MARK HUGHES
Manchester United

I KNOW I'm not the most skilful player in the game. Few would call me that. But nobody works harder than I do. And in the last two seasons I've found that, by putting myself about, I can hold my own in the First Division.

Hard work is something they didn't have to teach me when I came into football. It was the one thing I did know about, because I didn't make the grade as a footballer straight away.

For years I was a jack-of-all-trades. Coalman, window-cleaner, painter, road-worker — I had a go at everything. I stuck each of them for about a year before trying something else. I was just scratching around for a pound note. Mind you, I enjoyed most of them.

Cleaning windows was good fun. I worked with a few other lads. We had our own round, and charged 40p a go. With splitting the cash a few ways we had to do quite a lot of houses to earn any profit. But we had lots of laughs. We used to look for rain clouds — first sign of a drop we'd stop and go to the 'caff'.

The job that did most for me was coal-carrying. That's where I built myself up. Humping sacks of coal around makes you strong. I got pretty fit doing that job.

I'd be up before six every morning, load up five tons on the lorry, deliver them, and go back to the depot for another five tons. My lifting technique wasn't bad after a year

In the end I packed it in, because it left me too tired to play football. I used to work all Saturday morning before playing, and it wasn't helping my game.

Working for a living like that taught me a lot. It didn't do me any harm that's for sure. But you can't beat football. That's the best job I've ever had.

I appreciate it all the more because of my background. I put a lot into my football, but I don't really consider it work. I love it.

GOLDEN GOAL

A S a young kid I always wanted to be a footballer, but it didn't work out. I was slung out of West Ham, and I still don't know why. I thought I was doing all right, but they must have felt I wasn't going to make the grade.

At the time, I didn't bother too much. I shrugged it off. But when I found out what it was like working your socks off for a few quid, I realised what a good life football is.

When I see kids taking things for granted at clubs, I feel like telling them, 'You don't know how well off you are, so work at it'.

It didn't do me any harm coming into football late. I know what it's all about. But there's not so many chances in the game now. Kids have to take them when they come.

I got lucky in the end. While I was working in my different jobs, I was also playing football as an amateur in the East End of London. I didn't

YING COAL WAS JUST THE JOB

Millwall's TERRY HURLOCK Explains Why

make it at Enfield, so I joined Leytonstone and Ilford, and was spotted by Brentford.

I was nearly 22 before making my League debut, but since then I've not looked back. It's been great. The crowning part was playing for the England B team on tour in Europe last year.

Playing for England was a great experience, especially at the age of 30.

But it didn't give me big ideas. I didn't fool myself that I could get into the full squad, even if people were putting my name forward at one time. It was nice just to get the chance to represent my country for the first time.

I will treasure the memories — in particular the goal I scored in Iceland. That's one to look back on. But I always knew I didn't have an international future. I have never had any illusions.

But it was interesting to play for the England B team because of the different style of play. It was a total change from what I was used to. International football is all about possession.

The back four get the ball from the 'keeper, pass it on to the midfield and move it around. It was all new to me. I've always been used to a more direct style. But I enjoyed it, and I think I proved I could play that way, too.

Basically I'm still the same player I always was. I haven't really changed my game since I was in the Third Division.

People have always tagged me as a 'Hard Man'. I hate that. I don't go along with that image. It suggests I go around kicking people, which I don't. I've always considered myself as a hard worker, not a hard man. And maybe, among the hard work, there's a bit of skill as well. I can play a bit of football.

At top level you have to give one hundred percent to earn the right to show your skills. You can't go out and expect to be given room to show how good you are. But I'm not afraid of anybody. I go out and try my best, just as I've been doing for eleven years.

At Millwall we were a bit overawed at first by the thought of playing against the big names in the First Division. But once you get among them you realise they are not much better players than you.

There are no supermen in football. Every player's got only two arms and two legs, and if you work hard at shutting them down, there's not a lot they can do about it.

Millwall is a great club. I love the Den and the people. The fans are a joy to play for. They earned a bad reputation once, but they were never as black as they were painted. There's a great feeling at the Den. It's a club with a family atmosphere.

The club keeps in touch with the man on the terraces. They like to keep the fans involved, to encourage support from the community.

I think I'm the type of player the supporters appreciate. I get stuck in and give everything I've got.

People said we'd be outclassed in the top flight, but I think we proved a lot of doubters wrong. We may not have been taken seriously at the start, but at least we forced the other teams to sit up and take notice.

It was lovely to see the club's name at the top of the First Division table. It didn't last long unfortunately and we ended up being relegated. But I felt we'd given it our best shot — and you can't ask for more than that!

MARK BRIGHT
Crystal Palace

32

DAVID ROCASTLE *Arsenal*

Chris Waddle played his first match for Olympique Marseille last season, then threw his sweat-stained kit in a heap on the dressing-room floor — as he had done after every match in nine years with Newcastle United and Tottenham.

Hours later, Chris's playing strip was still there — nobody had told the £4.5 million signing that he had to wash his own kit!

That was one of the big shocks experienced by the England star on arrival in France. Things are done differently on the continent.

Just about every League club in England employs somebody to look after the team's kit — even if it's only a part-time laundry-woman with an old washing machine.

There may be the occasional Fourth Division outfit whose players take care of their own gear, but not many. And none of them would have paid over four million quid for a player to do his own washing!

Spurs believe in nothing but the best for the players — and for the playing kit. They employ two full-time kit men to get the best out of both.

Roy Reyland has been Kit Manager at Tottenham for the past five years. He is one of the busiest men at White Hart Lane.

"The job entails ordering the playing strip, boots, tracksuits and training gear for the players and coaches, and getting it ready for training sessions and matches," reveals Roy.

"Each of the 65 players at Tottenham has three sets of playing strip and three sets of training kit.

"We have our own laundry-room at White Hart Lane where three ladies work five mornings a week washing up to 150 sets of kit a day. Pre-season, and at some other times, players will use two lots of training kit each day."

Roy Reyland's average day starts at 7.30 in the morning, when he arrives at White Hart Lane. On Monday he'll unpack all the playing strips from the previous Saturday's game, sort them out, and give them to the laundry girls to wash.

Then he will sort through all the boots, cleaning and repairing where necessary.

Just before nine he sets out with the club van to drive to the training ground at Mill Hill with that day's training kit — prepared on the Friday. He lays out all the training kit for the players and coaches, and talks to the coaches about any special requirements for the day.

By 10.15 Roy is on his way back to White Hart Lane. The rest of the morning he spends cleaning and repairing boots.

In the afternoon he gets the freshly-laundered training kit sorted out and prepared for the next day's training. And if there is a mid-week match, all the kit for that has to be got ready.

If it is an away game, that means checking on the other team's colours to make sure there will be no clash, and then packing three full sets of playing strip. That means two full sets of short-sleeved shirts, and one set of long-sleeved shirts. Plus an extra set of different coloured shorts and socks as a safeguard.

"Some players wait to see what the weather and conditions are like before deciding on the shirt they'll wear, but there are some who will always wear one type," explains Roy.

"For example, Steve Sedgley, David Howells and Mitchell Thomas will always wear long-sleeves even if it's 90 degrees out on the pitch. While Pat Van den Hauwe, Gary Mabbutt and Paul Stewart wear short sleeves even with snow on the ground.

"We have to cater for everybody, but at least they all wear the same regular-size shirts. Shorts start from size 34 and range up to 40 — but I won't say who wears those!

"At away games involving an overnight stop, I'm always up early in the morning to go to the ground to check on playing conditions. If there has been a lot of rain we might need to fit longer studs to all the boots."

An essential part of the kit is Roy's 'box of tricks' for repairing boots. It contains various tools like screwdrivers, hacksaws and knives for dealing with emergencies.

"Sometimes aluminium studs can get rusted in, and when you try to unscrew them, the whole fitment turns," says Roy.

"I remember a match at Chelsea when one of the lads came in from the pre-match warm-up wanting a change of studs. I got a 'turner'. The stud wouldn't come out, and time was creeping on towards kick-off. It was time to panic.

"Out came the hacksaw, and I took the whole lot off, and managed to patch up the boot just in time. Nowadays I smear a little grease on the aluminium studs to stop them from rusting in — one of the tricks of the trade.

"One or two players like to look after their own boots, but most are happy to let me take care of them. In the old days it was a job that was

IT'S SO HECTIC!

A LOOK AT THE BUSY SCHEDULE OF SPURS KIT MANAGER ROY REYLAND

LAUNDRY CHECKS, KIT INSPECTION AND BOOT REPA — IT'S ALL IN A DAY'S WORK FOR ROY.

given to apprentices but now we prefer to do the pros' boots ourselves. If there's a tear or split we can repair it, whereas an apprentice wouldn't know what to do.

"In the minutes before kick-off time, there's generally a lot of tension in the dressing-room. Players have their rituals — dressing in the same spot, at a certain time, and in a particular order.

"Gary Mabbutt is very superstitious. He always puts his gear on in a certain way," reveals Roy. "You have to be careful to fit in with the players' requirement, and understand the pressures they're under.

"I remember one match when before kick-off Paul Gascoigne was moaning about his shorts saying how terrible he felt in them.

"I promised to sort it out, and took the shorts from him. I went out of his sight, waited a few seconds, then took the same pair of shorts back, and gave them to Gazza.

"He put them on and said, 'Great, Roy. These are just perfect!' You have to humour players before a match. I will always do what they want, even if it means changing a shirt 100 times, just to keep them happy."

Foreign trips — like pre-season tours — create the biggest headaches for Roy Reyland. Sometimes Spurs will play in three different countries on one trip.

"Those trips can be very hard. It's impossible to take enough fresh gear to get us through," explains Roy. "I ring the hotels we are staying at, to make sure there are laundry facilities to handle all our kit.

"Some seasons there are added problems when a change of design to the match strip means every item has to be replaced. That means a huge order to the manufacturers.

"We do have an interest in our own kit firm, Hummel, but it's still a major job to order a complete new set of

gear. We also order all the boots for the younger players, and any of the seniors who don't have individual contracts with manufacturers.

"Another part of my job is looking after the footballs. On home match days that means inflating three new balls to the right pressure.

"After one first team game, the balls are used by the reserves for one or two games, and then passed on to the youth team. After that they are used for training.

"We have around 60 footballs for use at the training ground, and another 40 for the indoor training area at White Hart Lane."

Shin-pads, ankle protectors and other strappings are also Roy Reyland's responsibility. Again, different players have different pads, with Spanish star Nayim favouring tiny, light-weight guards, while others prefer full-length pads. All these, too, have to be washed or wiped clean, and dried after matches.

One player at White Hart Lane poses a special problem for the kit manager. He's goalkeeper Erik Thorstvedt, the Norwegian international.

'Erik the Viking' is 6 ft. 4 in. tall, with a very long body. Standard size jerseys leave him with a bare mid-riff.

"We have to have goalkeeping jerseys specially made for Erik, eight inches longer than regular size," explains Roy. "Otherwise he would look ridiculous.

"Erik throws his gloves into the crowd every time we win, but for once, replacing them is not a job for me — he has an individual sponsorship deal with a manufacturer.

"Just about everything else that's worn by the players and coaches is down to me to look after. In season, it can be a seven-days-a-week job.

"But I love it. Tottenham is my club. And they are the best."

PRESSURE!

Some may think that being manager of Liverpool is an easy job. Lots of top players to pick a team from, plenty of money to strengthen the team — it's a situation most managers dream about. But as these pictures show, Kenny Dalglish is under just as much stress and strain as any other manager as he watches his team battle it out on the pitch.

GERAINT WILLIAMS *Derby*

SSSSHH! LADS — YOU'LL WAKEN UP THEIR DEFENCE!

Looks as if Spurs' striker GARY LINEKER is making a plea for silence, as he plans a stealthy raid on the opposition goal.

TELEPHONE TALK-IN

How ex-team-mates TREVOR PEAKE and STUART PEARCE keep in touch

Last season, less than 24 hours before Coventry City faced Nottingham Forest in their Littlewoods Cup semi-final, Highfield Road centre-back Trevor Peake phoned the man whose goal helped destroy his Wembley dream.

At the other end of the line, Forest left-back Stuart Pearce attempted to glean some up-to-date information from his former team-mate — and landlord.

The call is a weekly event. But when the two clubs clash, it takes on much greater significance.

Explains Peake, "Ever since Stuart left Coventry five seasons ago, we've had this ritual of speaking to each other on the night before match day.

"It's normally just general football chit-chat. But when we are due to meet, Stuart asks what we've done in training and the tactics we've been using.

"I normally tell him I'm not sure. Or say something to throw him off the scent!"

Peake and Pearce have been close friends since they signed for City during season 1983-84.

"We had non-League backgrounds — I was at Nuneaton, Stuart with Wealdstone — so we had a lot in common," Trevor recalls.

"At the start of the next term, I'd moved into a new house and Pearcey had left his rented accommodation. He arrived on the first day of pre-season training with his suitcases, and nowhere to go!

"I called my wife and she agreed to put him up for a couple of nights. He ended up staying for about eight weeks!

"Mind you, he was useful. Stuart is a qualified electrician and he did all our wiring.

"We've been firm mates ever since."

TREVOR PEAKE

IAN BUTTERWORTH *Norwich*

JOHN HENDRIE
Leeds United

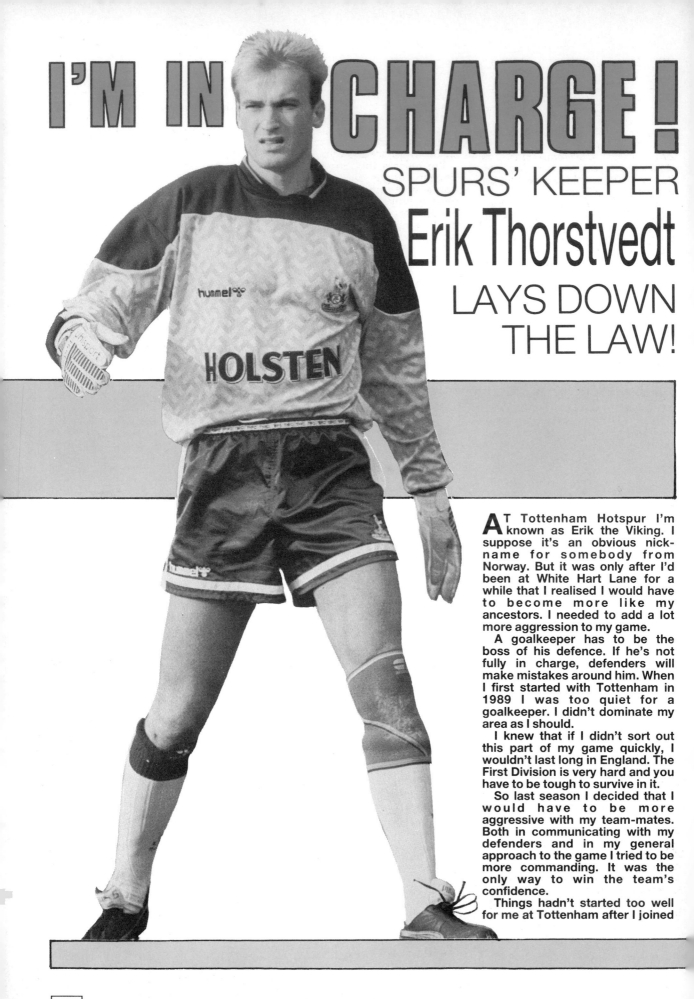

I'M IN CHARGE!

SPURS' KEEPER
Erik Thorstvedt
LAYS DOWN THE LAW!

AT Tottenham Hotspur I'm known as Erik the Viking. I suppose it's an obvious nickname for somebody from Norway. But it was only after I'd been at White Hart Lane for a while that I realised I would have to become more like my ancestors. I needed to add a lot more aggression to my game.

A goalkeeper has to be the boss of his defence. If he's not fully in charge, defenders will make mistakes around him. When I first started with Tottenham in 1989 I was too quiet for a goalkeeper. I didn't dominate my area as I should.

I knew that if I didn't sort out this part of my game quickly, I wouldn't last long in England. The First Division is very hard and you have to be tough to survive in it.

So last season I decided that I would have to be more aggressive with my team-mates. Both in communicating with my defenders and in my general approach to the game I tried to be more commanding. It was the only way to win the team's confidence.

Things hadn't started too well for me at Tottenham after I joined from Swedish club IFK Gothenburg.

It was just my luck that my first game for my new team was live on TV. Our opponents at White Hart Lane were Nottingham Forest, whom I knew would be very difficult to beat.

Unfortunately, I made a terrible mistake in that game. A shot came in from Nigel Clough and I let it slip through my fingers to give away a really soft goal.

We went on to lose that game 2-1 and of course I felt responsible. If the TV viewers hadn't heard of me before, they certainly knew me after that game. It was a harsh reminder of just how difficult it was going to be for me in England. I would have to work hard to put things right.

One thing that helped me was the reaction of my team-mates. Of course they weren't too pleased about my error but they encouraged me to put it behind me. They kept faith in me when others would have held it against me for a long time.

That's certainly what would have happened at one of my previous clubs, Borussia Moenchengladbach. If I'd made that sort of mistake there the other players would have all been against me.

The players at Tottenham are much more together as a team. There's a terrific spirit amongst the lads. Everybody is very friendly and enjoys a laugh. I felt accepted immediately and that helped me settle down very quickly.

My wife Tove and our daughter Charlotte soon started to enjoy life in England. It also helped that I could speak the language quite well.

Coming to England and joining a club like Tottenham was a complete contrast to life with Gothenburg in Sweden or indeed Norway. The attitude to football in Scandinavia is much more relaxed.

There is only an amateur league in Norway and only some of the clubs are professional in Sweden.

It's a different matter at international level. Sweden qualified for the World Cup in Italy and will be hosting the European Championships in 1992.

My country Norway are improving all the time but we always seem to get tough draws in the various competitions. This time we're in a European championship group with Italy, USSR, Hungary and Cyprus.

I'm certain that playing in the English League can only help my game at international level. I've already played over 50 games for my country and, as I'm only 28, I'll be looking to add to that total while I'm in England.

I've learnt a lot about goalkeeping in the time I've been in this country. Being here has certainly made me a better player.

I know that Tottenham have a great tradition of goalkeepers such as Pat Jennings and Ray Clemence seeing them through the 60's, 70's and 80's. Now it's my job to get them through the first few years of the 90's.

When I made that blunder against Nottingham Forest I don't suppose that too many Spurs fans thought I would last long. But thankfully, I gradually got them on my side. My form steadily improved and I helped the team climb to a respectable League position by the end of my first season.

VITAL ELEMENT

IN the summer of 1989 I had to have an operation on my knee that had been giving me a bit of trouble. While I was recovering from that I had time to think about my game. It was then I decided that the vital element missing in my game was aggression.

So when I got back into full training, I set about introducing it in to my game. I felt different straight away.

By the time the season had started I felt much more confident and positive about things. It certainly helped me to develop a stronger understanding with the back four, which is vital to any goalkeeper.

The fans must have recognised the difference, too, because they voted me their 'Player of the Year'. That was a terrific surprise, but a great honour, especially for an overseas player like myself. It was very important to me to be accepted by the Tottenham fans. They couldn't have given me a greater accolade than that award.

It was the evidence I needed to show I was doing the right things for the team. I'd done my best to cut mistakes to a minimum and the fans clearly appreciated that.

Who would have guessed that a year that had started so disastrously would end so well for me? Now I want to keep showing that the fans were right to choose me in front of all the other great players at Tottenham.

Unfortunately, I couldn't savour that moment for long. I hurt my knee soon after in a collision with Everton striker Graeme Sharp and was on the sidelines for a few weeks.

By the time I got back we were out of the FA Cup. Then Nottingham Forest knocked us out of the Littlewoods Cup. I think they must be my bogey team.

A season that had looked so promising had abruptly come to a disappointing end. It just showed how quickly things can happen in football. So I haven't won anything with Tottenham yet. But I'm sure it won't be too long before there is a medal of some sort on its way.

I quickly discovered just how difficult it is to win trophies in England. With a club like Tottenham, and with talented team-mates like Gary Lineker and Paul Gascoigne, I don't think I'll be kept waiting long for my first taste of success.

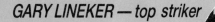
GARY LINEKER — top striker

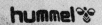

COLIN CLARKE
Ex-Queen's Park Rangers

ROBERT FLECK
Norwich City

MY TRANSFER WAS A REAL LIFE SAVER

Chelsea's KEN MONKOU explains why.

WHEN I joined Chelsea last year from Dutch side Feyenoord, I was looking only to save my football career. But as it turned out I saved my life as well!

Before joining Chelsea I had signed up for a trip back to my home country of Surinam in the summer. Surinam is a Dutch colony and a lot of players from there play professionally in Holland. Each year a group return home for an invitation match.

However, Chelsea had arranged a tour in Spain, and manager Bobby Campbell wanted me along to get used to the other players. I was upset at the time, but when you sign a contract you have to stick to the terms, and I understood Chelsea's position.

So instead of flying to Surinam, I flew to Spain with Chelsea. And that's what saved my life. The aircraft taking the Dutch footballers to South America crashed. 174 people, including the 23 players were killed. I would have been among them if I had not pulled out of the trip at the last minute.

It wasn't until after I got back from Spain with Chelsea, that I found out about the disaster. I rang my mother from the airport, and she told me about the crash. A lot of my friends were killed. My feelings were very mixed. I felt very lucky to be alive, but very, very sad about the deaths of so many people.

A few months later, Chelsea gave me permission to go back to Holland to take part in a testimonial match in memory of those killed in the crash. I played for a team of Surinam-born players against the Dutch national side and we won 2-1.

Joining Chelsea certainly saved my life, and I believe it has done a great deal for my football career. I have improved a lot as a player since coming to England.

I feel that the English League is the toughest in the world. If you can hold your own in England, I think you can play anywhere.

The Italian League is probably the most skilful, with many of the world's best players in Italy. But English football is the hardest. It is physically tough, and fast, but also more skilful than foreign people believe. I don't think English football gets the credit it should for its skill factor.

Most people on the continent underestimate the ability of English players. There are a lot of very good players here. I'm very pleased to have been able to establish myself in a top side.

I came to England to make a name for myself. I feel if I can succeed here, I'll have come through my biggest test. It wasn't possible to do it in Holland. At Feynoord I was in the same position as a number of young players who came through the youth team.

Because we hadn't cost the club a transfer fee we had to give way to big-money signings. If a player cost a lot he would always get in the team ahead of a youngster. It was very frustrating. I felt I was playing well, but I wasn't able to establish myself in the team.

But again I was lucky. Chelsea were interested in the Feyenoord striker David Mitchell, the Australian international. They watched him several times, and in doing so they noticed me. I feel I have proved a point to Feyenoord that I am capable of playing first-team football.

I am contracted for another two years at Stamford Bridge, and I want to make the most of that time to develop my game. I think I have adapted well so far to the English style.

Chelsea is a very good club to play for. The crowd is wonderful. Sometimes our away matches are like home games because the travelling Chelsea fans make so much noise. It's so unlike Holland, where crowds are much smaller than in England. In England every game is a big match. In Holland there are only a few tough matches for the big teams.

One of the hardest things to adjust to in England was that with the various cup competitions plus league games, we were playing two tough matches almost every week. Now I like it. I would rather play matches than train.

In Holland the training is longer. The clubs train twice a day instead of just in the mornings as in England. There is more work with the ball.

Last season was memorable for me because I played at Wembley for the first time. It was in the Zenith Data Systems Cup final against Middlesbrough.

People may think it a minor competition, but for me it was a very big occasion. It is the ambition of every foreign player to appear at Wembley. It's the most famous stadium in the world.

There is no comparable occasion in Holland to a Wembley Cup Final. The Dutch Cup is taken quite seriously, but the final is played at different grounds so it doesn't have the atmosphere of an English final.

There was a crowd of over 76,000 that day at Wembley and the atmosphere was fantastic. The game wasn't a classic, but we won 1-0, and I have my first medal from English football tucked away. I certainly made the most of my day out at Wembley. I hope it was the first of many visits with Chelsea.

Things have happened quickly for me in football, because I am only 25 now, and I didn't become a professional until I was 20 years old. I am pleased to have done it that way.

After leaving school I worked for a few years as a model, which I enjoyed. But it was the freedom to do what I wanted that was best. I was able to do all the things that young men enjoy doing — but which the discipline of being a professional footballer makes more difficult. I was able to get all that out of my system before I took up football.

I know about life outside the game, and now I'm happy to accept the discipline of being a professional. Young boys who become footballers straight from school

BOBBY CAMPBELL — Chelsea manager.

sometimes have trouble settling down, but I have avoided those problems. Twenty is not too old to start as a professional if you have the basic ability and dedication.

I hope to maintain my progress to earn a full cap for Holland. I'd love to follow in the footsteps of players like Ruud Gullit and Frank Rijkaard, who are both from Surinam.

I earned good reports for my appearance in the testimonial match last season, and I know the management of the Dutch team have watched me a few times in England.

I would describe myself as a marking centre-back who can also play a bit. In defence you have to mark players, but when the chance is there to come out of defence with the ball, I like to do so.

At the start of last season, Chelsea played with a sweeper. It was okay at first, but I don't think we really mastered the system. After a very bad patch, when we let in a lot of goals, we switched to a normal back four, and that suits me better. Our defensive record after that was very good.

My game has made a lot of progress in the last year since joining Chelsea. In every way I couldn't have made a better move!

CLIVE ALLEN
Manchester City

NIGEL CLOUGH
Nottingham Forest

IT'S BEEN A SEE-SAW

HOWARD KENDALL

FOR Manchester City's versatile young star Paul Lake, last season was a roller-coaster of ups and downs.

Newly promoted to the First Division, Paul and the other City players were eager to establish their club in the top flight.

But by December, City were deep in relegation trouble. It was an unhappy time for everyone at Maine Road.

As Paul explains, "Halfway through the season we were bottom of the table. The infuriating thing was that we weren't playing badly. We'd be dominating games and looking set for a win when suddenly we'd fall for a couple of sucker punches and find ourselves two goals down.

"Heads dropped. No way were we going to come back. A feeling of helplessness came over the team. Wherever you went in the club, there was an atmosphere of gloom and despondency.

"It wasn't manager Mel Machin's fault. To be honest, I think we needed a fresh face — somebody who would inject a spark of life into the side.

"New manager Howard Kendall did exactly that. Every player was lifted by his enthusiasm and the positive spirit he brought to Maine Road."

That boost helped open an exciting possibility for Paul when he was invited by Bobby Robson to join an England squad get-together at Lilleshall in January.

Adds Paul, "I knew my game had been below standard. But as soon as the new manager arrived, everybody's form picked up.

"If he decided to change the team, each of us was determined he wouldn't be the one to give way.

"It was this motivation which, I'm sure, contributed to my call-up to the England squad.

"I reckon I also benefited from playing several matches in London after rediscovering my form. Bobby Robson and his coaches probably had a good look at me and saw something they liked.

"It was a complete shock, however, when I found out I'd been called up. I was in London for an FA Cup replay against Millwall when I phoned home.

"My brother Michael, who plays for Sheffield United, had broken his leg against Ipswich Town the previous Saturday and I wanted to ask how he was. When he said I'd been invited to Lilleshall, I have to admit I thought he was winding me up."

DISTINCTION

PAUL'S delight was combined with a feeling of relief that he'd achieved this distinction despite a developing reputation for being injury-prone during international weeks.

Appendicitis, a twisted ankle, and other knocks had been responsible for his absence from four Under-21 and England B matches during the past two years. Even England manager Robson had expressed concern over Lake's record.

The player himself is reminded regularly of his persistent call-offs, and is annoyed that so much importance is attached to his bad luck.

"The get-together was mainly for fitness checks, and I think that was one of the main reasons Mr Robson wanted me there. I know he was concerned about my record of call-offs," says Paul.

"It's not through choice I've had to miss matches. If I've been unfit just before an international, I couldn't help it.

"I've even taken a knock on the ankle during the last few minutes of a match on the Saturday, it has swollen up, and that has been enough for City to rule me out of international duty.

"I can't blame the club when that happens. They must put themselves first. But it annoys me when people talk about my record as though it has something to do with my attitude. That's nonsense.

"It's pleasing to know Under-21 boss Dave Sexton has always kept faith with me. He knows I give my best every time I pull on an England jersey. And, for the same reason, it gave me a real lift to be included with the senior players."

Honoured though he was by his inclusion in the England get-together, Lake is also proud of the achievements of some of his young City team-mates.

"I think people must acknowledge that the so-called 'kids' at Maine Road have finally grown up," he goes on. "That has taken a long time in coming. I'm glad — for all of our sakes — that something has happened at last which will force everybody in football to realise we have matured into senior players.

"For the last couple of years, whenever things were going well, fans and the media would be saying what a great future City had because of the 'kids' breaking through.

"Yet, if we suffered a bad spell, the same people would give our lack of experience as the main reason.

"They didn't seem to realise that those who came through the ranks together are now more than 21 years old and most have four years' League experience. We're not kids any more.

"Steve Redmond and David White in particular are proving they are not only very good players, but very good First Division performers.

"Just because I'm the first one to be included in a senior England get-together does not mean I'm the best of the bunch. I don't believe I am.

SEASON -

for Manchester City's PAUL LAKE

"I'm just fortunate in having the bonus of being able to play in different positions. I'm sure it won't be long before a few of my mates are also knocking on the door."

Lake acknowledges, too, the importance of his bond with those five team-mates, and the fear they harboured that their association was in danger of being ended.

He explains, "There's a strong camaraderie among us. Steve, David, Andy Hinchcliffe, Ian Brightwell, Jason Beckford and myself have been close friends since we were ten years old.

"We progressed through the various teams before finally making it to the senior ranks. We have helped each other along the way.

"When there was a change of manager this season, we were apprehensive our bond might be broken.

"As soon as Howard Kendall arrived, he was linked with a number of players in the transfer market. We realised that, in order to bring in new men, he would have to sell others. We were worried our positions were under threat.

"Fortunately, the worry was only temporary. We've survived the buying and selling and been reassured by the manager that we have a future at the club.

"I think we all realise that if we go on giving 100 per cent, the boss can have no reason to move us on.

"We feel we can only benefit from the changes he has made. The team is better for the experience of the older players who've been bought.

"We believe our luck has changed. The only direction the team will move from now on is upwards," Paul closes.

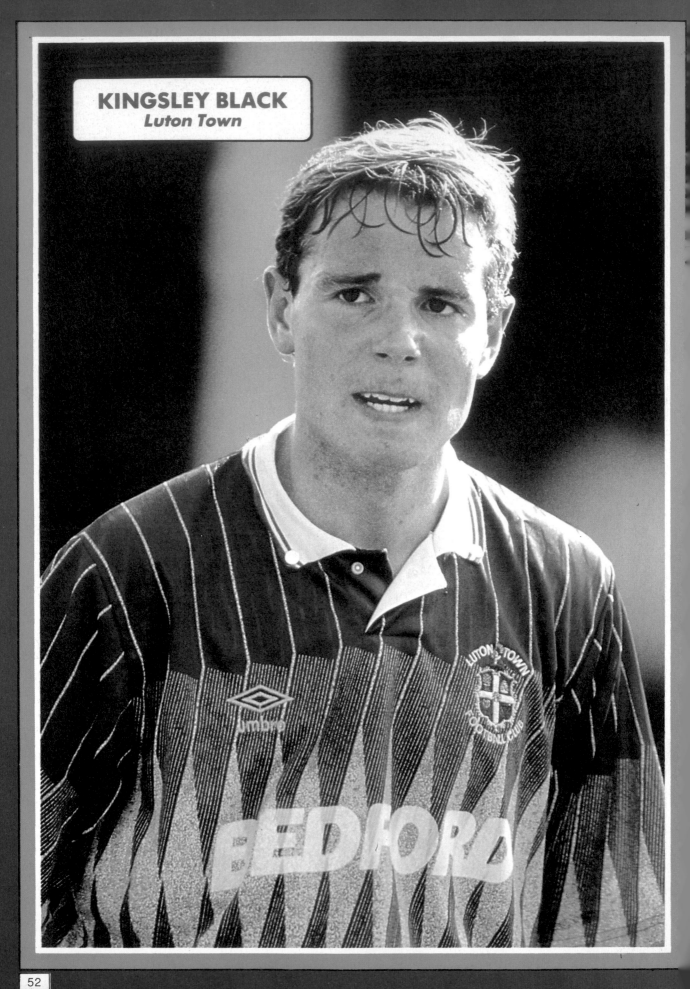

KINGSLEY BLACK
Luton Town

MICK QUINN
Newcastle United

53

JOHN ROBERTSON *Hearts*

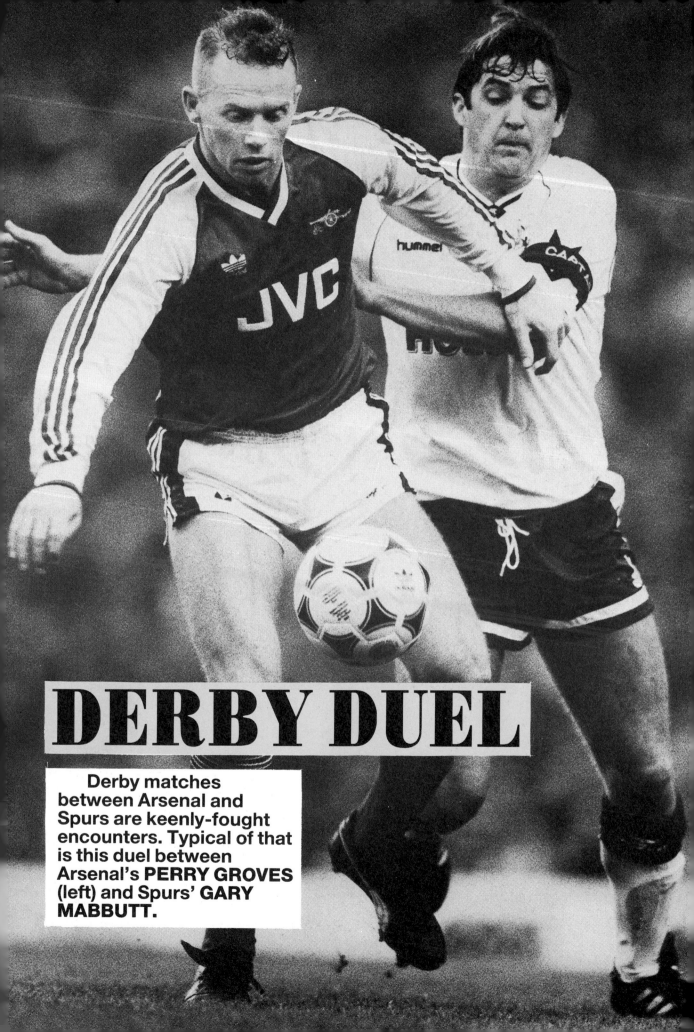

DERBY DUEL

Derby matches between Arsenal and Spurs are keenly-fought encounters. Typical of that is this duel between Arsenal's **PERRY GROVES** (left) and Spurs' **GARY MABBUTT.**

STEVE OGRIZOVIC
Coventry City

GARY GILLESPIE *Liverpool*

MY RANGERS

Ibrox star JOHN BROWN can't believe it's all come true.

IT was a dream come true when I joined Rangers from Dundee in January 1988. Becoming a Rangers player was the best thing that ever happened to me. Perhaps that's because I'd been a fan since I was a youngster and had a burning desire to play for the Ibrox outfit some day.

Throughout my professional career, I still dreamt of playing for Rangers. But, when Graeme Souness became manager, I honestly believed my chance had gone as he only seemed interested in signing big-names.

However, when I was approached with the possibility of signing for Rangers, I didn't have to think twice about accepting.

I had my idea of what Ibrox would be like. But, on arriving there, I have to admit I was taken aback by the sheer size of the entire operation. Still, in saying that, the atmosphere is very relaxed and everyone gets on well.

Ibrox is full of characters, so there's never a dull moment. Guys like Ian Durrant and Ally McCoist always keep you on your toes and, more often than not, in stitches!

It's people like McCoist, Mo Johnston and Terry Butcher who tend to be put in the limelight on the park and have to cope with lots of attention off it. That doesn't bother me as it allows me to get on with my job.

In my opinion, one of the least heralded players in the side was our best and most consistent performer last season — Stuart Munro. So, remaining out of the spotlight most of the time may not be such a bad thing.

However, if you do play for what is probably the country's biggest club, there's bound to be a little bit of pressure on you off the park. For example, people may bump into you in the street and want to shake your hand and talk for a while. As far as I see it, every Ibrox player is a representative of Rangers Football Club and must behave accordingly on and off the field.

CONSISTENCY

I've been shifted around the line-up without managing to settle into one particular position, but everyone seems to be relatively happy with what I'm doing.

Obviously, if I did get regular outings in the same spot, I'd be able to get more consistency into my game. But the main thing is, I'm getting a first-team place for the best side in Scotland.

That's a position I'm perfectly happy with, and that's why I signed a new three-year contract in the middle of last season.

A lot of people said we were just the best of a bad lot when we lifted the League Championship. But I'm afraid I can't agree with their reasoning.

It was always going to be tough for us last term. Every side in the Premier League raises their game against Rangers as, being brutally frank, they are jealous of the money Graeme Souness has at his disposal.

When Souness first arrived on the Scottish scene, I was with Dundee and I could sense that, within the club, everyone wanted to take Rangers down a peg or two. Consequently, all the players put in that extra effort and raised their game to try to come out on top. I did it myself — and I was a Rangers supporter!

The records will show that, last season, we sneaked a high percentage of our matches by a single goal. What they fail to show, however, is that we had most of the play in the majority of them and, at times, faced sides who were intent on playing defensive football against us.

We would find eleven opponents facing us when trying to get forward and mount an attack. It was obvious that certain teams went out against us determined not to lose the points.

Those negative tactics could account for the relatively small number of goals we scored in lifting the title last season. Nevertheless, we proved that, whilst a side can remain tight at the back, they can also place the emphasis on attack.

Unfortunately, certain sides didn't follow our lead. Especially when coming to Ibrox. We did go through a lean spell towards the end. But, at the same time, Aberdeen and Hearts were also dropping points. Over the piece, I felt we were worthy champions.

Of course, the Scottish Cup was a different kettle of fish. Celtic raised their game against us in the fourth round and, in the end, probably deserved to win what was a very disappointing encounter.

Whilst confidence was high in the build-up to that particular match, what we at Ibrox have to concentrate on is getting ourselves properly built for every single fixture — not just the big ones.

Generally, we have no problem getting in the right mood for games against the likes of Celtic and Aberdeen. But, when facing lesser sides such as Raith and St Johnstone in the Scottish Cup, it can be difficult.

That was shown in the tournament of two years ago. Raith came close to beating us in the early stages and, in the semi-final at Parkhead, St Johnstone could easily have ended up as victors!

It's getting that attitude exactly right which could be the key to lifting the Scottish Cup, the only domestic trophy which has eluded us since Graeme Souness took charge.

We're desperate to win the cup and I am positive we will rectifiy

DREAM!

that situation soon. As the boss maintains, however, winning the League and clinching that European Cup place is the main priority.

Admittedly, we were well beaten by Bayern Munich in the first round of the European tournament last season. But we suffered a lot of injuries and suspensions in the run-up to that match. If we could just avoid that, and gain a reasonable draw, there's a good chance we could make a lasting impression on the European scene.

There's no question we definitely have the necessary strength and talent in our pool to do just that.

STUART MUNRO — consistent performer

HIGH STEPPERS!

Aston Villa's **KENT NEILSEN** (left) and **DAVID HIRST** (Sheffield Wednesday) battle for possession.

KENNY SANSOM *Q.P.R.*

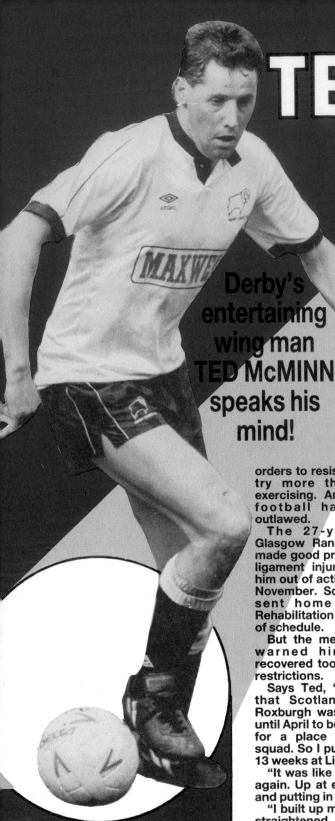

TED'S LEGS TELL THE TALE!

Derby's entertaining wing man TED McMINN speaks his mind!

TED McMINN ended last season acting as a ball boy in Derby County's practice matches. It was all the winger could do to stop himself from running straight on to the pitch at the club's training ground, and joining in the action.

But though he was full of running, and looked and felt as fit as a fiddle, Ted was under strict orders to resist the temptation to try more than running and exercising. Anything resembling football had been totally outlawed.

The 27-year-old former Glasgow Rangers favourite had made good progress from a knee ligament injury which had kept him out of action since the end of November. So much so he was sent home from Lilleshall Rehabilitation Centre well ahead of schedule.

But the medics at the centre warned him that he had recovered too quickly, hence the restrictions.

Says Ted, "I'd heard rumours that Scotland manager Andy Roxburgh was going to give me until April to be fit and challenging for a place in the World Cup squad. So I pushed myself during 13 weeks at Lilleshall.

"It was like being back at work again. Up at eight every morning and putting in a full day.

"I built up my leg so well, it had straightened out much quicker than anybody had expected. I was doing running and step-up exercises which other players with the same injury weren't doing until a month later.

"I'd originally been booked in to attend Lilleshall during the summer, but I came on so quickly that they sent me home a couple of months before the end of the season and told me I could report for just two days a week.

"However, all my hard work was to no avail. The physios told me I'd built the leg up too quickly and, despite feeling so fit, I still had to wait the recommended six months before playing again.

"What they said made sense. Even though my leg as a whole was strong, the ligaments which had been damaged hadn't been given enough time to recover. If I made my comeback too early and went in for a heavy tackle, I could easily have torn them again. And the medics stressed that they couldn't just keep on repairing them.

"I got over the frustration of knowing that it was too late for the World Cup, but the last few weeks of the season were dreadful.

"When I turned up at the training ground the rest of the lads would be playing in a practice match while I was restricted to running round the pitch. I'd stop and watch, hoping that the ball would go out of play near me just so that I could run after it and kick it back.

"I was just torturing myself. It felt as though I had a new toy, but somebody kept taking it away from me.

"I trained throughout the close-season so that I was ready for the start of this term."

For the long-legged winger coping with injury is no new experience. When he returned from a year in Spain with Seville, his legs looked more like those of a battle-scarred infantryman rather than a top class footballer.

A weal here, a row of stitch-marks there. Elsewhere a still-unhealed gash or a bruise the size of a fist. Hardly a square-inch of flesh which didn't tell the story of an unsavoury encounter with a Spanish defender.

Said Ted, "When I arrived at Derby and underwent my first examination, physiotherapist Gordon Guthrie couldn't believe it.

"At that time, I had a long, freshly-made gash under each knee. There were clear imprints of studs up and down my legs.

"Gordon said he had never seen anything like it in all his years of dealing with sports injuries.

"One of the other Derby players told me, 'You look as though you've been attacked by a shark!'"

Those souvenirs were the only legacies of a Spanish experience which McMinn brought back with him, and which he carried around for quite some time. The rest, apart from the sunshine, he was happy to leave behind.

He goes on, "When I went to play for Seville towards the end of 1986, I was optimistic about performing well over there.

"I was following my old Rangers boss, Jock Wallace, who'd been such a big influence on me during my time at Ibrox.

"I was confident I would continue benefiting from working under him and was sure I'd enjoy playing in the Spanish League.

"For a while it worked out fine. Regular fixtures against the likes of Barcelona, Real Madrid and Bilbao were a bit like playing in the European Cup every week. I enjoyed that.

"But long before I returned to Britain, things had started to go wrong.

"Jock was sacked, a victim of the pressure imposed by players who didn't like his style.

"I was left on my own, ignored by team-mates who resented me. Nor did I get on with the Seville directors.

"Day by day, I was made to feel more and more alone. I knew that, very soon, I wouldn't be able to tolerate it any longer.

"When Derby manager Arthur Cox offered me the chance to come back to Britain, I had to accept.

"The only high note on which I left was that the Seville fans still thought the world of me. In that sense, I was still a winner when I departed.

"If it had been any other way, I would probably still be there, plugging away, trying to be a success. That's the way I am. I would never have given up before making the grade. I'd have packed in only when I was ahead.

"In fact, the fans loved me from the moment I pulled on a Seville jersey. I do daft things on the field, and I think I entertained them straight away."

English fans who saw television clips of McMinn while he was playing for Rangers will know exactly what he means.

His gangling manner and the spidery stretch of a leg to rescue an over-hit ball as he drags it past defenders, often has a comical look about it.

"The Seville fans went for that in a big way," says Ted, "but they also appreciated my willingness to run at opponents.

"I don't think they had seen that very often, and it made a refreshing change for them.

"However, it definitely didn't go down well with opponents. Spanish defenders don't take kindly to someone dribbling his way past them.

"On the majority of occasions when I went past someone, I received an elbow in the face, a row of studs crashing into my shins, or I had my ankles clattered. Hence the collection of scars which decorate my legs.

"If that was all I'd had to contend with, however, I'd simply have regarded it as an occupational hazard and carried on with the job.

"While Jock was there, everything else went well. In retrospect, maybe too well. The pair of us helped one another settle in our new environment. Even away from the club we spent most of our spare time in each other's company.

"We tried to learn Spanish, but didn't know enough of the language to speak freely to the locals.

"As time passed, we became closer. In fact, our relationship was a bit like that of a father and son."

ARTHUR COX

"In the end, I think I paid for that. There were signs of things to come even before Jock left.

"When we travelled to away matches, the rest of the players had their little get-togethers. Jock and I were never invited to them.

"After Jock was sacked, most of the players treated me like a leper. Perhaps it was my punishment for being what they considered a manager's pet while Jock was in charge.

"More than likely it was because I was a foreigner and, therefore, an outsider.

"There were a few exceptions. Team-mate Ricardo Sera shared a room with me on club trips. We gave each other lessons in our respective languages and remained good friends.

"I was even taken advantage of by the new manager. Because I was the only player prepared to switch to a new position, I was always the one who had to do so if someone was injured.

"Spanish players think of themselves as being a specialist in one position, and refuse to play anywhere else.

"When it came to the crunch, I couldn't tell the team-boss, 'I was signed as a winger and that's where I'm staying.' That just isn't done in the football circles in which I was reared.

"Another bone of contention was the payment of wages. The players were paid annually — a system I had difficulty getting used to.

"By the time the end of my last year approached and money was due, I had terrible trouble getting the club to shell out.

"What with one problem piling on top of another, I felt it was time to go."

Having been placed on the open-to-offers list, McMinn had the chance to sign for Bayern Munich. Newcastle United were also interested.

But he chose Derby because he'd been so impressed by manager Arthur Cox and managing director Stuart Webb.

"Having met Mr Cox, my first reaction was to liken him to Jock Wallace in his no-nonsense approach. That convinced me I'd enjoy playing for him," said Ted.

"I feel I've made the right decision. Compared with those last few months in Spain, my arrival at Derby was a bit like being welcomed back into my own family.

"And you'll never know how big a relief it was to team up with players who actually speak the same language as me," Ted closes.

JOHN BURRIDGE *Newcastle United*

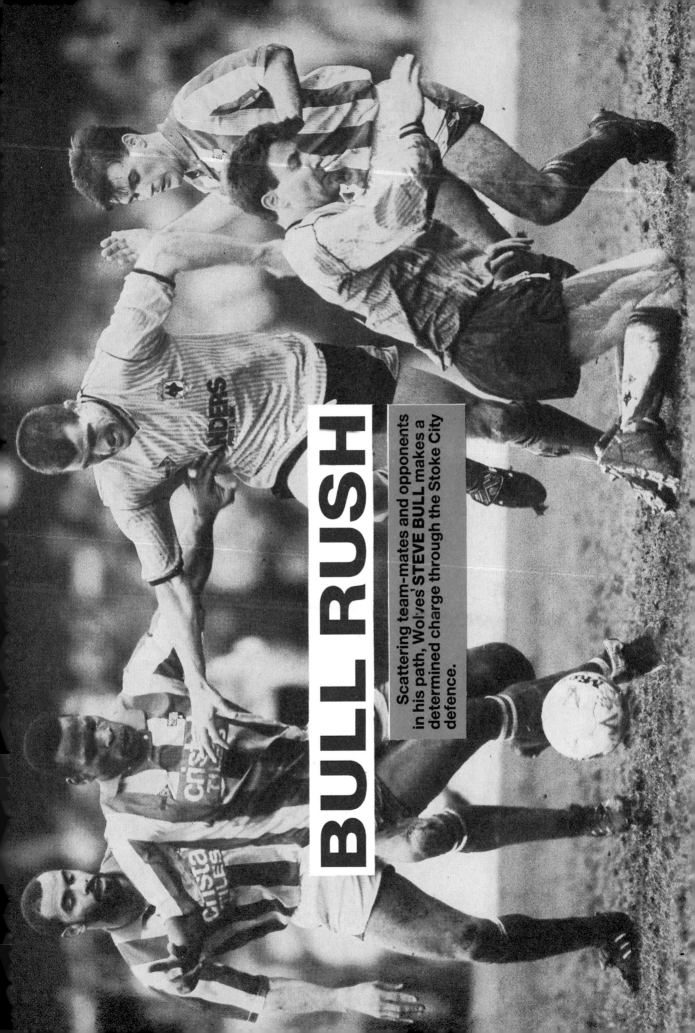

BULL RUSH

Scattering team-mates and opponents in his path, Wolves' **STEVE BULL** makes a determined charge through the Stoke City defence.

IF there's one thing harder than winning a place in the Liverpool first team — it's hanging on to it!

Young left-back Dave Burrows will agree with that. He and Steve Staunton have vied for possession of the number three jersey since David joined the Anfield club from West Bromwich Albion in 1988.

Neither has been dropped in favour of the other. One has played until he has been injured, then had to wait until his rival has been crocked.

As David himself says, "I definitely feel we are of equal ability at the moment. As long as the one in the team plays up to standard, he will probably stay in.

"We both know the score. We are good friends. The only rivalry is strictly a professional one. And we never discuss the situation when in each other's company.

"But it does mean you try to stay in the side at all costs," Burrows continues. "I must admit I played when I shouldn't have done before a hamstring went on me.

"I'd been feeling it for a couple of weeks, but carried on. That sort of strain, however, will find you out at First Division level. I took the risk and it didn't pay off.

"I was out for two or three games. By the time I was fit, Steve was doing well and I had to wait.

"When I first joined the club an injury crisis meant I got almost immediate first-team action. I didn't really experience what it's like at this club to battle for a place. But I know now what it's all about!

"There are two players for every position. And of the current line-up I'm the only one who hasn't won a full cap.

"I don't have an inferiority complex about that, but I did have one during my early months at Anfield," admits Burrows.

"I hardly said a word for ages. Certainly wouldn't dream of saying anything out of line. I was overawed at being in the same squad as a player like Alan Hansen, who has achieved so much.

"I've overcome that initial reaction, but I'm still very reluctant to criticise senior players unless it's over something obvious.

"That might change, I don't know. Normally I'm not one to hold back. I feel much more settled at Anfield now, but I'm still very much a learner.

"The Liverpool players are amongst the best in the world. If they don't know what the game is all about, nobody does.

"So I try to concentrate on doing my job right. I'm working hard and I feel I'm already a better player than I was last year.

"I certainly feel I'm improving. I'm picking things up all the time. Most notably, I'm now saving a lot of energy by using my head.

"When I first played for Liverpool I was charging about all over the place. But you very rarely see a Liverpool player exhausted. They work hard, but in the right places. And they use their brains. I feel I'm starting to do that."

What Burrows is also doing now is showing the confidence to ignore some of the 'instructions' issued by the Liverpool bench during matches!

"Young players often seem to take the brunt of the shouts from managers and coaches during games," he points out. "It's the same at any club. The more experienced lads are left to get on with it.

"Also being a full-back, I'm usually positioned close enough to the touchline to become a 'target'. And the staff at Anfield are known to be pretty vocal during games.

HESITANT

"When I first came into the side I was listening to their shouts as I received the ball and was also hearing calls from team-mates. In addition I probably had it in my own mind to do something entirely different.

"The outcome was that I was sometimes hesitant on the ball, not knowing which instruction to follow.

"Now I've gained enough confidence to make up my own mind in most situations. Obviously I still listen to what's being shouted from the touchline, but it no longer creates indecision in my play.

"The gaffer, Kenny Dalglish, is helping me to come to terms with the 'play-it-and-move' game which Liverpool have always adopted. It's a system which everybody must fit into.

"I'm much more involved in attacks than I was with West Brom. There, we were a struggling side and much of my work was defensive.

"I'd say I now spend 60-70 per cent of a match in the opposition half. That means improving the quality of my crosses.

"It's my job to place the ball into areas of greatest danger. I know strikers such as Ian Rush and Peter Beardsley will be on the end of the service I provide."

In front of Dave in the Anfield line-up is John Barnes, and the youngster has discovered that fitting in with the winger's special talents has been a major priority.

"I had to work at building up an understanding with John," says the full-back. "Basically, it was up to me to adapt to his style, not him to mine.

"He is the one who's in the England team, so the way he plays is bound to be right.

"We got in each other's way at first. I was running into his space and stopping him going down the line. Now our understanding is much better.

"John is also making me look a good player. I might still take up wrong positions, but he's so skilful he'll make sure I receive the ball. I see a lot of it and John is my main supplier."

Burrows confesses he is unlikely to have ever reached his current level of achievement without the influence of former England star, Nobby Stiles, who was coach with West Bromwich Albion.

"Nobby is the best bloke I've ever worked for," Dave enthuses. "He played such a big part in keeping my head from dropping when successive Albion bosses kept leaving me out of the first team.

"Nobby was mostly in charge

of the reserves during my time at the Hawthorns, and he would lift me when I felt low — and that was quite often as I always seemed to be the one left out.

"He kept stressing that I was a good player, that I must keep working hard, and I would be given another opportunity."

Burrows' transfer to Merseyside came within hours of him making his debut for the England Under-21 side against Sweden at Coventry.

He is the first Liverpool player to appear regularly at that level since Sammy Lee back in the early 80's. Very rarely do the Anfield club field anyone as young as Burrows in their established first team.

"Meeting up with the Under-21's does me a power of good," adds Dave. "I'm with players of my own age so there's no feeling of being intimidated, as there has been at times with Liverpool.

"Quite the reverse, in fact. I feel I'm treated with just a little bit more respect because I'm a Liverpool player. That is great for personal confidence.

"But I'm taking nothing for granted. That's one thing you soon learn if you play for Liverpool."

IT'S TOUGH AT THE KOP!

Liverpool's young star DAVE BURROWS can vouch for that!

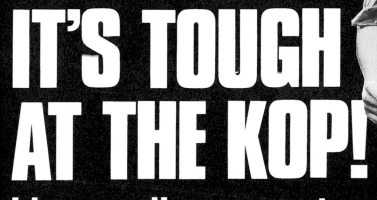

STEVE STAUNTON

67

NIGEL SPINKS *Aston Villa*

WHY DOES EVERYBODY CALL ME 'FAT BOY'?

Spurs star PAUL GASCOIGNE seems to have the evidence to prove there's not a lot of weight in what his critics say!

ARE YOU LOT DEAF?

Rangers and England 'keeper CHRIS WOODS marshalls his defence in parade ground style

JOHN FASHANU *Wimbledon*

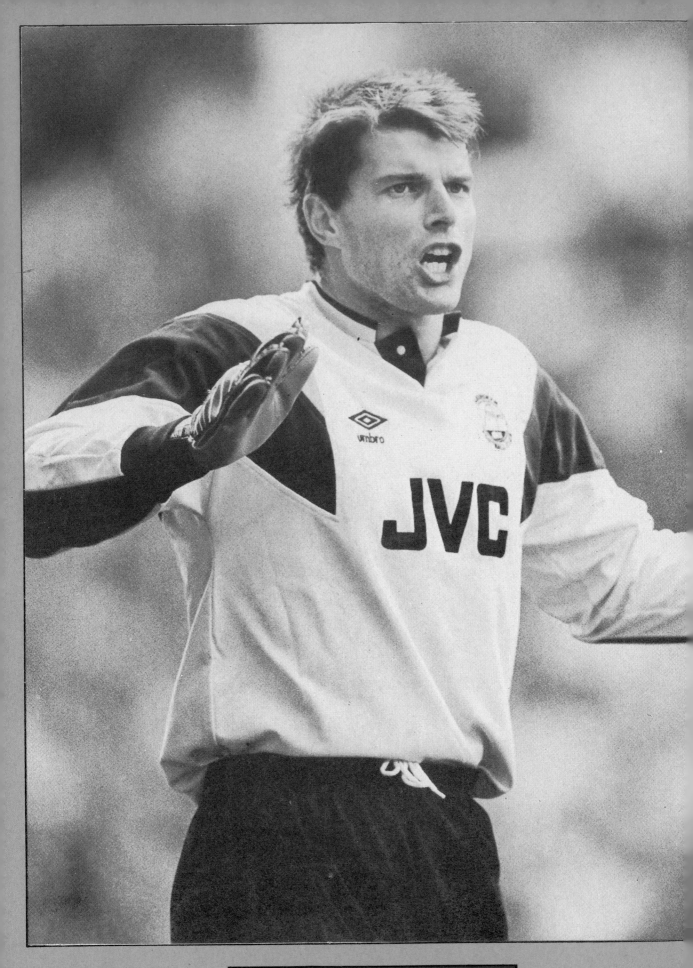

THEO SNELDERS *Aberdeen*

DAVID SPEEDIE
Coventry City

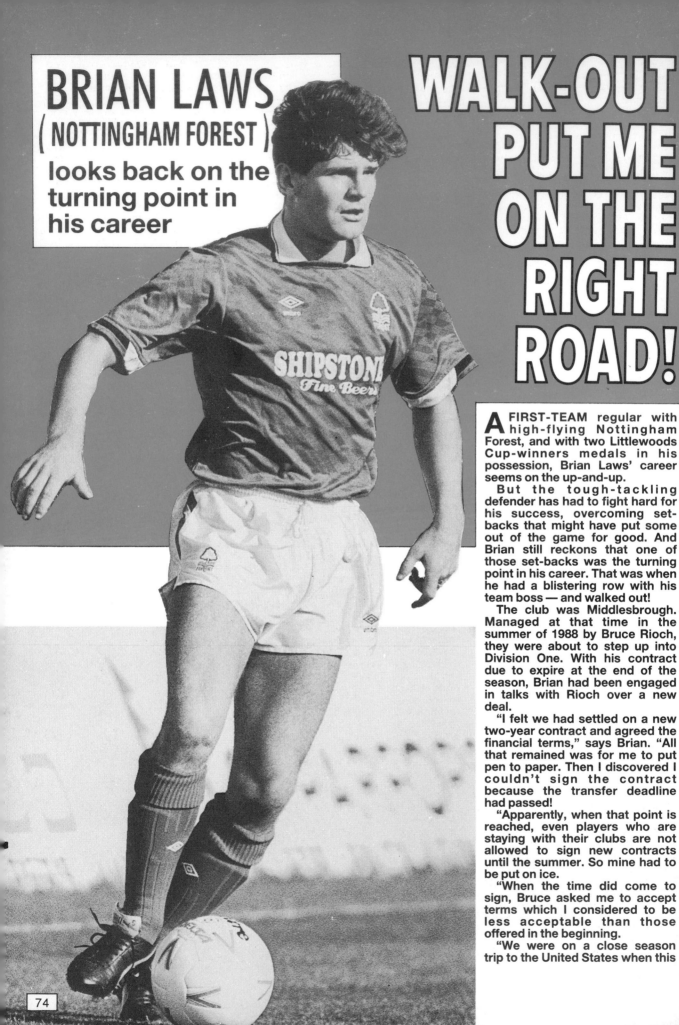

BRIAN LAWS (NOTTINGHAM FOREST)
looks back on the turning point in his career

WALK-OUT PUT ME ON THE RIGHT ROAD!

A FIRST-TEAM regular with high-flying Nottingham Forest, and with two Littlewoods Cup-winners medals in his possession, Brian Laws' career seems on the up-and-up.

But the tough-tackling defender has had to fight hard for his success, overcoming set-backs that might have put some out of the game for good. And Brian still reckons that one of those set-backs was the turning point in his career. That was when he had a blistering row with his team boss — and walked out!

The club was Middlesbrough. Managed at that time in the summer of 1988 by Bruce Rioch, they were about to step up into Division One. With his contract due to expire at the end of the season, Brian had been engaged in talks with Rioch over a new deal.

"I felt we had settled on a new two-year contract and agreed the financial terms," says Brian. "All that remained was for me to put pen to paper. Then I discovered I couldn't sign the contract because the transfer deadline had passed!

"Apparently, when that point is reached, even players who are staying with their clubs are not allowed to sign new contracts until the summer. So mine had to be put on ice.

"When the time did come to sign, Bruce asked me to accept terms which I considered to be less acceptable than those offered in the beginning.

"We were on a close season trip to the United States when this happened. I told him there and then that once we arrived back in Britain I would never play for the club again.

"I did play in several tour matches, but I never gave more than 80 per cent effort, and Bruce Rioch knew it.

"Bruce told me he had decided he couldn't risk giving a two-year contract to a player who had suffered a serious knee injury such as the one which had kept me on the sidelines for seven months. Instead he could offer me only a one-year deal.

"In fact, I'd made a full recovery from the injury, and knew I'd done enough in the first team since my comeback to prove it.

"This was later borne out during the sitting of the transfer tribunal which was to set the fee for my move to Forest.

"Insurance company representatives told the tribunal that, once a player had made 15 consecutive appearances following injury, he was deemed to have made a full recovery. I had made 30."

Laws' first action, following his initial confrontation with Rioch, was to search for a new club.

He recalls, "From our base in the States, I telephoned my wife, Margaret, and dictated a letter which I asked her to send to most of the clubs in the First and Second Divisions.

"By the time I returned home 15 days later, six replies, all fairly encouraging, were waiting for me.

"In the end, I didn't speak to any of those clubs because there had been one other response to my letter — a telephone call from Nottingham Forest's assistant manager, Ron Fenton, saying his club would be interested.

"By the time I'd spoken to Forest, there was no need to consider anybody else. The main pull towards the City Ground was a desire to play for Brian Clough. I was at that stage of my career when I felt working under him could do me the world of good. So it has proved.

"I had two dreams in football. To play in the First Division and to appear at Wembley. I had achieved neither.

"The first I'd hoped to do with Middlesbrough. That wasn't to be, of course. Now, with Forest, I've done both, and as a bonus I've picked up two Littlewoods Cup-winners medals as well."

Laws believes it's a double achievement which he fully deserves after everything that has happened to him.

He reflects, "I've probably gone through every turmoil possible for a footballer. In fact, I feel as though I've banged my head against so many brick walls, I should have a broken nose!

"I was at Middlesbrough when the club sank into the Third Division and then went into the hands of the Official Receiver.

"I was one of the players who turned up for training one morning, only to find Ayresome Park locked and our entry barred.

"I stuck with the club through the financial crisis, continuing to play for them even though I went several months without receiving any wages. During those months, my mortgage wasn't being paid.

"Until the day arrived when the club recovered and my money started coming in again, I worried constantly about meeting my responsibility to my family. I knew too, how much worry it was causing Margaret.

"Having come through all that, I then went through agony with a knee injury. At one point I wondered whether it was to cost me my career."

Laws was struck down two years ago by damage to the anterior cruciate ligament of his right knee.

The operation to repair the damage was followed by months of slow and painful physiotherapy and training.

"I can remember lying in a hospital bed just after breaking down with the injury, and thinking about all those other players who'd been forced to retire after suffering similar injuries," says Brian.

"I wondered whether I might end up in the same boat. But it was only a fleeting thought. After that initial doubt, I never allowed myself to think negatively again.

"From the moment I emerged from the surgery, I never entertained the thought that I might not play again.

"I worked damned hard and put myself through a lot of pain as I battled for fitness.

"I spent 15 weeks away from my family at the Lilleshall Rehabilitation Centre, swimming and cycling my way to a full recovery.

"When I returned to first-team football and helped 'Boro win promotion, I knew all the pain was worth it.

"I still don't know how to properly thank the surgeon, Mr Muckle, for making my comeback possible. In my opinion, he performed a miracle.

"That he repaired my knee well enough for me to play again would have been sufficient. But I don't even have marks to show what I went through.

"I find that amazing when I see other players who have scars which look like zip fasteners!"

But even after all those battles, Brian still had a fight on his hands when he joined Forest.

As he explains, "Steve Chettle was the man in possession and Gary Fleming was his understudy. I had to get in line.

"Assistant manager Ron Fenton realised my frustration and kept telling me to be patient. He promised me my chance would come.

"After plugging away in the reserves I finally won a first team slot in December, 1989."

Brian Laws held that place as Forest won their way to Wembley for the Littlewoods Cup Final. Then disaster!

Only a week before his Wembley date, Brian was in hospital recovering from surgery to a hand injured in an accident at home. To make matters worse the player was kept in suspense by manager Brian Clough. He was told only a few hours before kick-off that he would line-up at Wembley.

Said Brian, "I was certain my hand would be OK and I knew the coaching staff and club physiotherapist had assured the boss I would be fine, but I didn't know how he would react.

"Once again this season Brian has been a Wembley winner, only this time there were no last minute injury scares to cope with!

Now he's keeping his fingers crossed that the ups and downs of the last few seasons are well and truly behind him

STEVE CHETTLE

SAFE AND SURE!

Nottingham Forest's **STEVE SUTTON** makes a clean catch to thwart Chelsea's **GORDON DURIE.**

TONY DALEY
Aston Villa

LAST season — my first at Old Trafford — wasn't an easy one, even though we ended the campaign on a high with our F.A. Cup victory.

During the term, however, the club had a lot of ups and downs — and so did I. Right from the start I was sure there were people just waiting for me to fall flat on my face.

Until I'd established myself, no matter how well I played, I knew it wasn't going to be good enough to earn rave reviews.

If I put in a good performance, then that was only to be expected from a £2.3 million player. If I was below par, I was slated. I got a bit of that during my opening spell at Old Trafford.

It didn't help that I made an unfortunate start. We lost 2-0 at home to Norwich City on my debut. I was blamed for their first goal, even though I didn't think it was all my fault, and I made a rash challenge on Robert Rosario which led to a penalty for their second.

The trouble was, a lot of people seemed to use that game to judge my showing over a period of matches, which gave totally the wrong impression.

I'd say I showed indifferent form. I put in a few bad games, but just as many good ones. Thankfully, the fans on the terraces didn't give me any stick. They were patient, and I appreciated that, because I desperately wanted to prove to them that the club had not blundered in gambling so much money on me.

It probably took me almost five months to feel that I'd truly settled in at Old Trafford. But I was never worried about being able to cope.

I knew exactly what lay ahead for me when I signed for the club. The sort of attention which Manchester United attract was one

made their initial bid.

I can tell you, I went from one emotional extreme to another, then back again, in the space of a week, without even being included in talks.

I'd had no personal contact with United by the time they made a bid of £1.9 million for me. But it didn't take long to build up my hopes of going to Old Trafford.

I knew that Middlesbrough were holding a Board meeting to consider the bid, and I sat at home impatiently waiting to hear their verdict. Then I heard on the radio that they'd turned down the offer.

I have to admit I was shattered. I'd been preparing myself to meet United for talks the next day. Suddenly, I was a Second Division player again.

The next week was the most dreadful of my life. I played three matches for Middlesbrough during that week, and felt the strangest sensation.

I was very aware of the fact that the 'Boro' fans were watching a player whom they knew wanted to leave the club. How could they give me their backing? That thought certainly affected my performances. I found it very hard to concentrate. Even keeping my mind on training was difficult.

My Mum and Dad helped take the pressure off me. I was still living at home, and they were brilliant. They kept telling me not to worry. If United wanted me so badly, they'd come back for me they reassured me. They were right of course.

Moving to United has also given me the chance to turn back the clock and make up for the disappointment of my one and only previous season as a First Division player.

I've had to prove myself again after being a member of the 'Boro'

IT WAS TOUGH!

Manchester United's big-money signing GARY PALLISTER looks back on his first season at Old Trafford.

of the reasons I set my heart on joining them. And I was fully aware, when I heard what they were paying for me, that it would increase the pressure.

But I'd already been through a similar experience with Middlesbrough, so I was used to being the focus of attention.

When I made my debut for England while playing in the Second Division, I was taught a few lessons on how to handle the pressure. At times I didn't cope with it too well, but I learned from the experience.

I found out then just what it was like to have people build you up, then be just as keen to shoot you down again.

I remember how I reacted to reports about my performances after I became an internationalist. When they were favourable, I let it go to my head. I made myself believe I'd cracked it — and I was only 22.

Then I'd play badly and get a panning, and I didn't know how to take it. I felt so low I'd let it affect me in other games.

So when I came to Old Trafford, I knew I was in for similar attention. But I had the experience to be able to put it to one side and plug away quietly until I'd bedded in.

I hadn't wanted to leave Middlesbrough. But when we were relegated to the Second Division, I had to think about my own future. I decided it was time for me to move on, hopefully to a bigger club. I went to see manager Bruce Rioch at the start of last term and told him how I felt. Though he didn't want me to leave, he understood, and told me to leave. Then Manchester United

side which was relegated after just one season in the top flight.

As an England internationalist, I was aware that so much was expected of me, and I was determined to live up to everybody's hopes. But even two matches for England didn't prepare me for the First Division.

We'd previously made the step-up from the Third to the Second and found there wasn't much difference. But this was another matter entirely.

The huge gap in standard took most of us by surprise. It was a lot faster, and you were punished for just about every mistake. Most of us just weren't prepared for it.

I made an unlucky start when I picked up an injury during pre-season training and missed the opening of the campaign. It was two months before I felt absolutely right.

Nevertheless I felt I hadn't done myself justice throughout the season and finished the campaign feeling that I'd let myself down. That's why last term meant so much to me. It's given me another chance to prove myself at the highest level. And one reason I think I can do it dates back to Willie Maddren, my first manager at Ayresome Park.

Having played in the same position as me, he helped a lot in developing my game and took me for special extra coaching sessions.

But the most important thing he gave me was belief in myself. I've handled everything that has come my way since joining United and I know I have the ability to reach the top — and stay there!

ROD WALLACE
Southampton

KERRY DIXON
Chelsea

AGONY!

Midfield general **GORDON STRACHAN** has taken a few knocks in his time. But no matter how experienced you are, hard knocks still hurt. Leeds star Gordon was in the wars against West Bromwich Albion.

KEVIN GALLAGHER *Coventry City*

CRASH LANDING!

Derby's DEAN SAUNDERS takes a tumble after a no-holds-barred tackle by CHRIS PRICE (Aston Villa).

PETER SHILTON
Derby County

RON ATKINSON — free transfer decision.

FOR SUCCESS...

BUT IT ALL STARTED WITH A FREE TRANSFER!

SPEARHEADING the honours chase of high-flying Aston Villa, pushing for an established place in the England team, David Platt is one of the brightest stars in the game.

Yet, only four years ago, it seemed his career had reached a dead end. He was in the manager's office at Manchester United and Ron Atkinson was telling him he was getting a free transfer. David Platt had no future at Old Trafford.

Although it was a shattering blow, the idea that he wasn't going to make it at Old Trafford hadn't been far from David Platt's mind. In the time since signing for United, he'd never progressed past the reserve team.

But it was none-the-less a kick in the teeth to the youngster who'd joined Manchester United at the age of 17 and who'd dreamt of making it with one of football's big names.

Instead, David Platt found himself one of the many free transfer men looking for a club. He found one all right, but turning out for Fourth Division Crewe was a far cry from high-flying Manchester United.

And it left David Platt with a confidence problem. He joined Crewe wondering if he was good enough to play in even Fourth Division football.

But gradually belief in his own

Close-up on the amazing career of Aston Villa's
DAVID PLATT

ability began to return and more importantly the goals began to flow. Soon the bigger clubs began to take an interest in Crewe's exciting young prospect. Among them was Aston Villa.

Eventually Villa manager Graham Taylor, after a final look, paid £200,000 for him in January, 1988.

At the time Villa were in the Second Division, but by the end of that season they had won a place in the First. David Platt had his part in securing promotion by playing in the last 11 games and picking up 5 crucial goals.

With Villa in the First Division, David continued to impress. He held down a regular place in the Villa first team, playing in all 38 League games. He also showed he could find the net in the top flight by finishing as the club's second top goal scorer, losing out only to Alan McInally.

But last term was to do even more to enhance David Platt's reputation. During the close

season McInally was transferred — and when the League programme began, David found himself being played as an out-and-out striker.

He immediately took to his new role and throughout the season he was in the top batch of goal-scorers. His goals — and overall play — were a vital factor in Aston Villa's challenge to lift the League title. While other more fancied contenders fell by the wayside, Villa battled it out with Liverpool right to the closing stages.

On the personal front David Platt's performances earned him an England call-up — and forced him into the reckoning for a World Cup place in Italy.

In some quarters, David Platt is seen as the future replacement for Bryan Robson in the England set-up. Although he has played mainly as a striker for Villa, he has expressed a preference for a midfield role.

Given his tremendous workrate, his eye for a goal, and his all-round skills, it's little wonder that some people see him as a Bryan Robson in the making.

But David Platt has done enough to earn star rating on his own achievements. A fact that was underlined when his fellow players voted him Player of the Year in 1990. Some performance for a former free transfer!

GRAHAM TAYLOR — talent spotter.

DAVID PLATT — on duty for England.

TOP MAN — David Platt with his Player of the Year trophy.

VINNIE SAMWAYS
Tottenham Hotspur

BATTLE OF THE BIG MEN!

Manchester United's GARY PALLISTER gets the better of Aston Villa's **TONY CASCARINO** in this high-jumping duel.

IT JUST FLEW BY!

Arsenal's LEE DIXON looks back at last season.

I JUST can't believe how quickly last season flew past. If they all go like that, I'll be retiring before I know where I am. But I had few complaints at the end of it, even if we had lost our championship trophy. Apart from that, nearly everything else went right for me.

Within the space of a few weeks in April, I'd been selected as the best right-back in the country by the Professional Footballers Association, my wife had given birth to our second baby, and then I was picked to play for England.

The PFA selection was very special because it meant other Division One players had considered me as the best of the bunch. As I'd previously been picked for the Second Division team when I was at Stoke, it was a satisfying double to complete.

Not long after that recognition, a couple of slices of luck went my way and I suddenly found myself in the England squad.

Firstly, Rangers' Gary Stevens picked up an injury that looked like knocking him out of the running for the game against Czechoslovakia. Then, the night before Bobby Robson was due to pick his squad, Paul Parker got himself sent off in a League game, which meant he wouldn't be able to play either.

That same night, Bobby Robson was at Highbury watching our game against Aston Villa. I was just one of several players he'd come to watch, but ironically I wasn't actually playing at right-back.

Because of a number of injuries, George Graham had drafted me into the midfield where I found myself marking another England player, Villa's David Platt, for most of the match.

Thankfully, that didn't do any damage to my international chances. In fact, it might have helped Bobby Robson knowing I had a bit of versatility about my game.

In any case, the next day I was named as the only regular right-back in the England squad. It looked odds-on that I would be playing against Czechoslovakia at Wembley the following week.

But there was precious little time to worry about that in between times because my wife was just about to give birth to our second baby, Oivia. It was hard to believe that all these things were happening at the same time.

Then the next week it was all rounded off in style when I played the whole of the Czechoslovakia game for England. I knew that it was still very unlikely that I would be going to the World Cup, but there was still plenty to play for.

I'd played for the B team before so I'd had a taste of the international scene, but that was nothing compared with the real thing.

It felt particularly good to be the only Arsenal player in the team. Several of the other lads were in the B team so I'd got one up on them on that occasion.

The game itself was very special. Paul Gascoigne had a great match, Steve Bull scored two goals and we ran out 4-2 winners.

From my own point of view, I thought I had quite a solid debut. It took a while to get settled but once I'd done that, I felt I played my part for the team.

It helped me a lot that night to be playing just behind Trevor Steven down the right flank. Coincidentally, I'd made my League debut in the same Burnley team as Trevor back in 1983.

That wasn't the best time to be making my debut. Burnley had a great year in the cup competitions, getting to the semi-finals of the Milk Cup and the quarter-finals of the FA Cup.

But in the League, they were already doomed to drop down to Division Three by the time I made my first appearance three games from the end of the season.

And I was to play only one more game the next season before manager John Bond called me into his office to give me some bad news. He said he had to let me go on a free transfer.

That showed me just how tough football was going to be and that I still had a lot to learn. It knocked me back a bit at the time.

I suppose I was still a bit young and raw at that stage in my career. There were a lot of rough edges to my game. My main problem was that I'd not been an apprentice anywhere. At 16, when most lads were joining their first clubs, I was signing on for an economics course at a local college.

Young players learn so much in those two years and I'd missed out on that side of my football education. I was playing for a local league team until I was 18.

After Burnley, my next stop was Chester. It was first-team football, but with a struggling side.

For most of the time I was there, they were near the bottom of Division Four. That was not what I wanted from football. I honestly thought I could do better for myself than that so I asked the manager for a move.

Now most people say that I was given another free transfer at that point. But that's not true. My new club, Third Division Bury had to pay £3,500 for me. It might not have been very much but at least some money changed hands. And with that move to Gigg Lane, my career started moving as well.

The boss there was my old Burnley team-mate, Martin Dobson. He was the one who really spotted some potential in my game.

Along with his assistant, Frank Casper, he started moulding me into a more all-round player. Their coaching obviously worked because, after just one season with Bury, I was moving upwards again to Second Division Stoke City.

At the Victoria Ground, I was to receive some more expert tuition from my new boss, Mick Mills. He'd played at full-back many times for England so I couldn't have had a better teacher.

By that stage I was beginning to feel much more confident in my own ability. I knew that eventually I would be playing in Division One.

That opportunity came when Arsenal signed me towards the end of just my second season at Stoke. But I wasn't given away on a free transfer this time.

There I was in the First Division with one of the biggest clubs in the country. It was all very different to life at Chester or Bury. But I didn't kid myself that just because I was at Arsenal I knew everything I quickly realised there was still a lot to learn.

From now on, I had to complete my education against the best players in the country. As a right-back that meant I was up against the best left-sided players around, including John Barnes.

Since I've been with Arsenal, I've had some great tussles with John. We've played some very important games against Liverpool in the last couple of seasons and keeping John quiet has always been a priority.

I knew that if I could do well against him, then I would have a fair chance against the others. John Barnes has so much skill, you never know what's coming next. I just try to keep my balance and not commit myself too early.

One false move against him and he'll punish you for it. He's a scorer as well as a provider, so there's always plenty to worry about.

When I made my England debut, I'd been hoping that he'd been in the team as well. It would have made a pleasant change to be on the same side, but unfortunately he was injured.

I always enjoy the challenge of playing against John Barnes. But it's only what I've learned from the Arsenal coaching staff that gives me a chance of competing on equal terms.

My first task when I arrived at Highbury was to learn the Arsenal way of defending. The basic principle of that is to force the attacking player inside so that he can't get to the line to get in a cross.

I have to admit that it took me a while to get used to life in Division One. That wasn't too surprising as I'd come up through the League so quickly. But I knew I would have to learn quickly to hold on to my place. A First Division team can't afford passengers.

There was one stage, halfway through that first full season, when the boss did leave me out for a few games.

I knew I'd been struggling a bit and getting lost with some of my positional play. Perhaps I needed to be dropped to get things right.

Thankfully, I missed just three games before I was called back in. After that, my confidence returned and I felt I was doing the job right at last.

Soon after, George Graham decided to change to a sweeper system instead of the traditional back-four. It was a gamble when we were going flat-out for the title but it proved to be the decision that won it for us.

The new system allowed myself and my full-back partner, Nigel Winterburn, time to push forward even more than before and that suited me fine.

It all came down to the final game of the season. We had to win by two goals at Liverpool to lift the championship.

I still have very strong memories of that remarkable Friday night and often re-live it all over again on video. Of course, there was no more memorable moment than when Michael Thomas scored the title-clincher a minute from the end.

It was difficult to take it all in at the time. Not long before, I'd been playing for a team propping up the rest of the League in Division Four and there I was picking up a championship medal.

The celebrations went on for the rest of that summer. But we were to come back down to earth at the start of the next season. We lost 4-1 against Manchester United at Old Trafford on the opening day. We realised then that it wouldn't be easy to defend the title.

In fact, the team never really got going all season, and we went on to finish fourth.

I still had a lot to be satisfied with though. While other players admitted they weren't at their best, I knew I'd developed considerably.

That England recognition at the end of the year convinced me there's still plenty to look forward to in the next few seasons. So I hope time doesn't flash by too quickly!

GEORGE GRAHAM

PAUL WILLIAMS *Charlton Athletic*

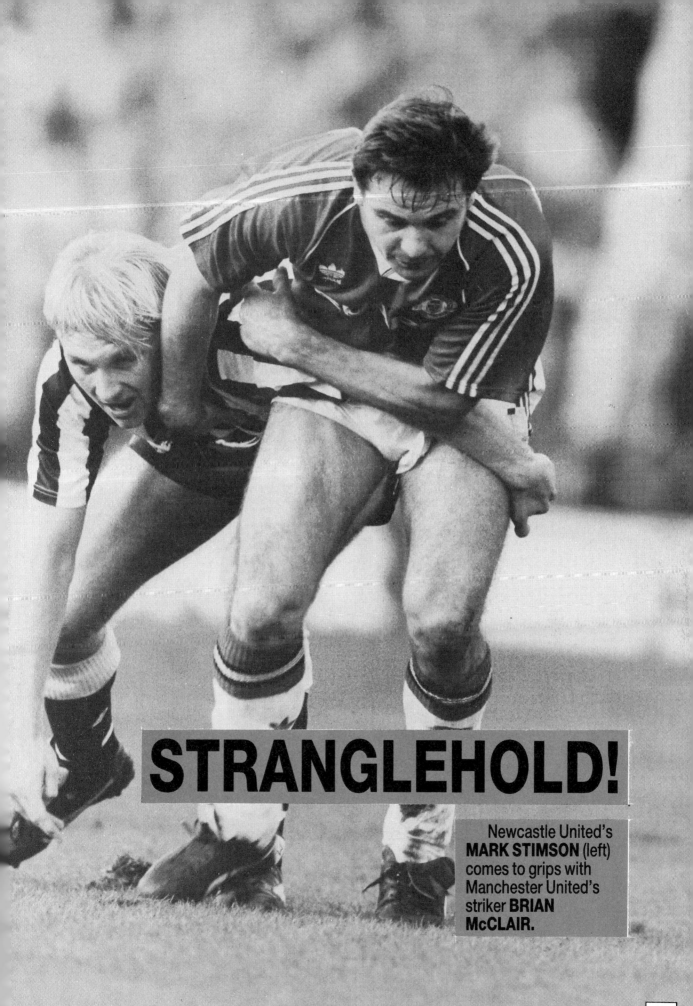

STRANGLEHOLD!

Newcastle United's **MARK STIMSON** (left) comes to grips with Manchester United's striker **BRIAN McCLAIR.**

IT'S IN THE BOOK!

Southampton's keeper TIM FLOWERS reveals his secrets

When you're a goalkeeper, there's always something new to learn about the game. To make sure I don't forget anything, I write everything down in a special book. It's really helped to improve my overall game.

It all came about when my ex-Wolves and Southampton clubmate, John Burridge, brought his own book into training when we were at Molineux together.

John led the training for the goalkeepers and before each session he would write down the routines on a piece of paper. He was constantly looking at it to see what came next.

When training was over, Budgie would take the piece of paper home and copy it all out into his special book. He would also make comments on how each of the exercises had worked.

He was an obsessive trainer. 'Keepers usually train longer and harder than outfield players,

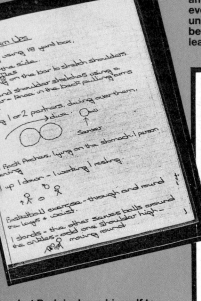

anyway, but Budgie drove himself to the limit. He isn't the biggest of 'keepers so he knew he had to work hard to overcome that. Some of the taller goalies, like Dave Beasant, hardly have to dive to make a save but Budgie has to keep that spring in his feet.

Another aspect of training that he introduced me to was weights. All-round body strength was very important to Budgie and he could certainly shift some big weights.

He was the right shape to cope with weights. I've got longer limbs, so I

have to use them in a different way.

When Budgie left Wolves in 1984, it gave me the chance to establish myself. I was only 17 but I'd had a good teacher to prepare me for life in Division Two.

What I didn't know at the time was that I'd be meeting up with John Burridge again, three years later at Southampton.

I originally went to the Dell as number two to Peter Shilton. It was a move that I knew just had to benefit my game, even if I didn't play for the first team. You don't say no to teaming-up with the best 'keeper in England.

Shilts was a very different sort of trainer to Budgie, but equally demanding. He concentrated on quality training rather than long-sessions and you can't argue with its results.

Peter expected those around him to be as professional as he was. That meant he wanted balls to be thrown in just the right place when you were helping him out with a training routine.

He would come down hard on anybody that upset his rhythm. It kept everybody on their toes. I was understudy to him for just a season before he moved on to Derby but I learnt a tremendous amount during

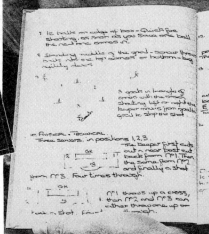

that year.

When he left I might have expected a chance in the first team myself, but then that man Burridge turned up. It was obviously disappointing to take second place, but I was more than happy to be back with John.

There's no secret about it. Budgie is

my hero and to this day I still get ribbed by the other lads about how much I go on about him. When we were reunited at the Dell, I was reminded about his book. I decided it was time to keep one myself.

For starters, I had to make a note of

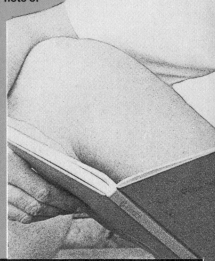

everything I'd learnt under Peter Shilton. I had no problems remembering it all because you just don't forget what Peter teaches you.

I wanted to make a note of all the different routines that either Peter or Budgie had

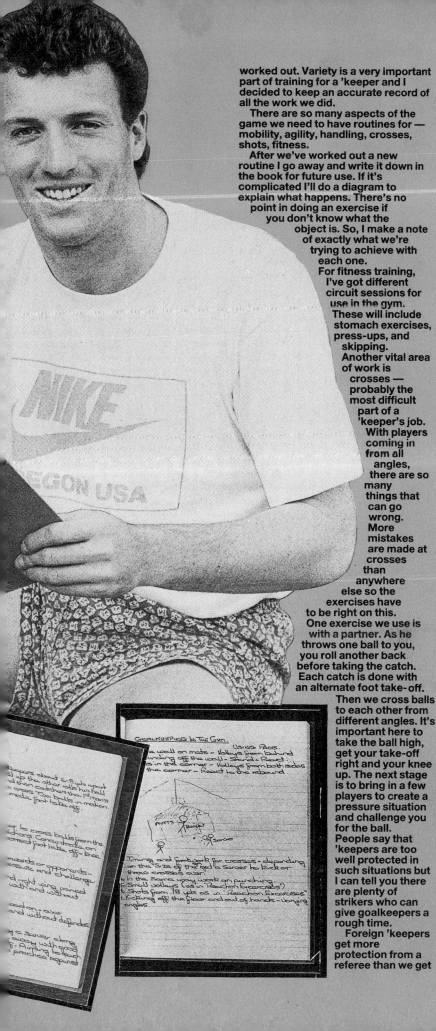

worked out. Variety is a very important part of training for a 'keeper and I decided to keep an accurate record of all the work we did.

There are so many aspects of the game we need to have routines for — mobility, agility, handling, crosses, shots, fitness.

After we've worked out a new routine I go away and write it down in the book for future use. If it's complicated I'll do a diagram to explain what happens. There's no point in doing an exercise if you don't know what the object is. So, I make a note of exactly what we're trying to achieve with each one.

For fitness training, I've got different circuit sessions for use in the gym. These will include stomach exercises, press-ups, and skipping.

Another vital area of work is crosses — probably the most difficult part of a 'keeper's job. With players coming in from all angles, there are so many things that can go wrong. More mistakes are made at crosses than anywhere else so the exercises have to be right on this.

One exercise we use is with a partner. As he throws one ball to you, you roll another back before taking the catch. Each catch is done with an alternate foot take-off.

Then we cross balls to each other from different angles. It's important here to take the ball high, get your take-off right and your knee up. The next stage is to bring in a few players to create a pressure situation and challenge you for the ball. People say that 'keepers are too well protected in such situations but I can tell you there are plenty of strikers who can give goalkeepers a rough time.

Foreign 'keepers get more protection from a referee than we get in England. But their first priority is to punch a cross, something that would be a last resort to me. But punching still needs to be practised. When I punch I'm aiming to put the ball right outside the box.

Corners and free-kicks are obviously very important to get right. We work on both near and far-post kicks, bringing in players again to put us under pressure.

Everytime anybody dreams up a new exercise I jot it down in the book. Despite all the hard work we do, some people still claim that goalkeepers make a lot of 'lucky' saves. But I can tell you that the 'lucky' ones are very rare.

When the ball is travelling at speed, positioning and reactions have to be spot-on. If the ball appears to hit a 'keeper, the chances are that it's because of his speed of thought and agility, and nothing to do with good fortune.

My goalkeeping 'bible' has become even more important to me since Budgie left Southampton last year and I got my chance to establish a regular place in the first-team. Everything I'd learnt came in to play at last.

I'd been patient for a long time but I knew last season was the crunch for me. If I hadn't got in the team then, I might have had to leave the club. Last season was a very exciting one to be in the team. Rod Wallace and Matthew le Tissier were knocking in the goals at one end but unfortunately they were going in at my end too.

I didn't blame myself for too many of them. We play an attacking type of game and I'm bound to concede a few goals.

Obviously it worries me when goals go in and some 'keepers will blame themselves for anything that gets past them. But the most important factor for me was that I was playing consistently well.

My performances are another thing I make a record of in my book. I tend not to be too hard on myself and give reasonable marks out of ten for most games.

I write down a few points about each game with particular reference to any penalties that are taken against me. I also look out for penalties that are taken on the TV. Every bit of information helps.

The book is something I intend to keep going throughout my career, especially as I'm now in charge of training routines with the 'keepers. That's no easy task. I'm still only 23 and the other senior 'keeper, Ian Andrews, is older than me and the other keepers aren't much younger.

Unfortunately, we don't have a specialist goalkeeping coach at Southampton. So last season I asked our boss, Chris Nicholl, if we could go up to the National Sports Centre at Lilleshall to work with England coach, Mike Kelly.

I'd worked with Mike with the England Under-21's and I knew he would do us a lot of good. He's one of the best coaches around. He worked us very hard but I think everybody benefited.

Of course, when we'd finished at Lilleshall, I had lots more to put in my 'bible'.

DARIUSZ DZIEKANOWSKI *Celtic*

SINGLE-MINDED

Getting to that ball first is the one thought of Arsenal's ALAN SMITH (left) and Everton's NEIL POINTON.

ARM IN ARM

Charlton's **CARL LEABURN** (left) joins forces with Manchester United's **MIKE DUXBURY** as they wait for the ball to arrive!

GARY THOMPSON *Crystal Palace*

A TOUCH OF LUXURY

The Good Life — Old Trafford Style.

DANNY McGREGOR

HOW would you fancy watching your football in the lap of luxury every week? And that doesn't mean sitting in front of the telly, with your feet warming by the fire as you tune into The Live Match.

To do it in real style, you have to roll up outside the main entrance of your local club, then spend a few hours relaxing in your private box overlooking the pitch. You'll have your select band of invited guests to keep you company, of course. The weather doesn't matter. You'll be snug in your heated room.

How about a spot of pre-match lunch? No need to move from your seat — a waiter brings your selection from a mouth-watering menu.

And once the match itself gets under way, you can celebrate every time your team scores by watching the goal again, thanks to the club's video service.

All this can be yours at every home match, if you are lucky enough to lease one of the fast-growing number of executive boxes installed at some of the country's top clubs.

Manchester United currently have 103 of them at Old Trafford, with plans to install a further batch in the next stage of ground development.

The club's commercial manager, Danny McGregor, is justifiably proud of the facilities and services provided by the club. And he pulls out all the stops to ensure that the V.I.P. fans are provided with everything they need.

Says Danny, "Manchester United poineered this type of spectating facility. Our first boxes were installed when the main stand was rebuilt in 1965 for the World Cup Finals the following year.

"Since then, we have regularly improved and added to them, and we like to believe that we provide the best such service in the country.

"It has certainly proved a very popular way of watching matches at Old Trafford. We have a waiting list for our boxes and it tends to be a long wait. They are leased by the season and last year only one box was given up.

"We have plans to develop the Stretford End of the stadium, and hope to include a number of boxes, maybe even a double tier of them. When that happens, we will have no shortage of takers."

United currently have 95 five-seater boxes and 8 eight-seaters. Each is comfortably fitted with heater and television. Each box also has a fridge — handy for keeping your champagne nicely chilled.

Most are leased by companies, who use them for entertaining clients, but a small number are held by individuals.

A guest lucky enough to be invited to watch a United match from one of these prime spots could never say he wasn't looked after, from the moment he drives up to Old Trafford.

Adds Danny, "We have 16 acres of car parking space at Old Trafford, and the box-holders have the prime location — right outside the ground. It's just a few steps to the main reception or the private-box entrance.

"Guests are greeted by a uniformed commissionaire, who hands them a programme and directs them to their private box.

"Alternatively they can head for one of many bars to meet friends and relax over a drink. There is a bar exclusively for box-holders.

"However, most arrive between one and two o'clock, go straight to their box and order lunch.

"Though they eat in their box, we like to think it is just like dining in a top restaurant. The food is of the best quality and we provide top waiter service.

"We also have our own television channel, and on every home match day we put on a video of a previous United game.

"We also use our video facilities to put on a live showing of the match being played, complete with action replays of any dramatic moments.

"There's no hurry to leave after the match is over. We are happy to continue serving drinks and coffees for those who prefer to wait until the traffic has cleared."

By then, Danny himself will have made an appearance at each box, ensuring that everybody has been well looked after.

He goes on, "On matchdays, I'm on duty at Old Trafford from 10 am until about 7 pm, and spend part of that time doing a round of the boxes.

"Our members like to receive the personal touch so, catering manager Michael Wheton, ground manager Dominic McCormack and myself like to visit them personally.

"We do encourage the box holders to let us know if anything is not quite right. We always try to rectify things immediately.

"But, though there is the occasional complaint, we must be doing something right, because the boxes are always full," points out Danny.

MANCHESTER UNITED
Executive Suite
Special Matchday Lunch

£15.25
per person inclusive

Cauliflower Soup
Melon & Ginger Barquet
Smoked Chicken, Celeriac
& Cucumber Salad
Deep Fried Scampi
& Plaice Goujons

Roast Beef & Yorkshire Pudding
Escalopes of Pork Fillet
in Mushroom Sauce
Poached Fillet of Lemon Sole
with Lobster Sauce
Pot Roast Pheasant with Vegetables

Chef's Selection of Vegetables

Sweet from the Trolley
Cheese Selection

Coffee

Price includes VAT & Service Charge
SHARP
ELECTRONICS (UK) LTD.

THAT'S MY BALL!

Determination and a spring-heeled leap make sure MICK HARFORD (Derby) comes out on top in this clash with TIM SHERWOOD (Norwich).

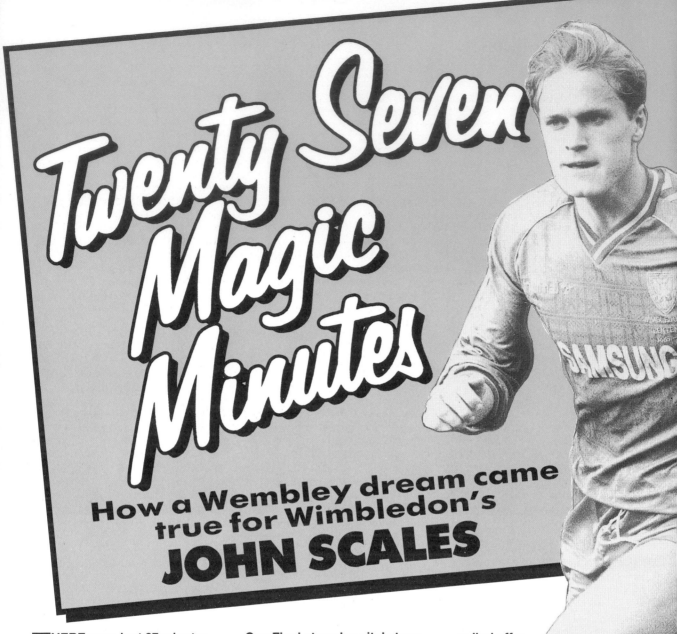

Twenty Seven Magic Minutes

How a Wembley dream came true for Wimbledon's JOHN SCALES

THERE were just 27 minutes remaining in the 1988 FA Cup Final between Wimbledon and Liverpool when I got my chance to play on the famous Wembley turf.

Two minutes earlier Dave Beasant had made his famous save to stop John Aldridge's penalty and protect our 1-0 lead.

Now the boss, Bobby Gould, called me over and asked me to do a particular job for him. He was going to take striker Terry Gibson off and he wanted me to play up front in his place.

The fans probably thought it was a strange decision. Why was Bobby playing a full-back at centre-forward?

What they didn't know was that I'd actually started my career as a striker with Leeds United. So coming on in the FA Cup Final at such a vital stage was a test of memory, as well as my ability.

I don't think the boss was really expecting me to score a second goal. He just wanted me to run my legs off for 27 minutes.

So there I was running around trying to make life difficult for the Liverpool central-defenders — Gary Gillespie and Alan Hansen. They start so many of Liverpool's attacking moves and I had to break that down.

To be honest, I don't think I touched the ball more than a couple of times but I probably ran several miles in the process.

When the final whistle went I certainly felt as if I'd been playing in a match but it was worth the effort.

As usual, Wimbledon had confounded the critics and pulled off a surprise. We'd beaten the League Champions and nobody could quite believe it.

Winning the FA Cup was not something I could ever have expected after my start in football at Leeds. But that had certainly given me a good introduction to the game.

When I was at school in Harrogate, football was just one of the sports I played, along with rugby and athletics.

At 17, I still had no idea that I would make football my career. In fact, I was probably more interested in architecture then. Houses and building of all types have always fascinated me and I would love to have studied the subject properly.

That ambition was put on hold though after Leeds spotted me playing in the North Yorkshire Under-19's trials. They asked me to go to Elland Road on a non-contract basis and I agreed.

Leeds had always been my team and I wasn't going to turn down this opportunity to join them. They might have been going through a transitional stage but it was still a great place to be.

Eddie Gray was the manager at that time and players like his brother Frank, Peter Lorimer and David Harvey were still around.

There were also a lot of good young players who were to make their names elsewhere, such as Scott Sellars (Blackburn), Denis Irwin (Oldham), Tommy Wright (Leicester), John Sheridan (Sheffield Wednesday), David Linighan (Ipswich), Andy Linighan (Norwich), Terry Phelan (Wimbledon) and David Mehew (Bristol Rovers).

I started off there as a right-winger but, for what turned out to be my last six months at Elland Road, I moved to full back.

That all happened because in the six-a-side training games, everybody realised I was better at defending than attacking. That was where I eventually got a run in the reserve team, although I never actually made it to the first team.

Then it was all over. Leeds released me and for a while it looked as if my football career was finished. It was a terrible disappointment to be rejected by the club.

Luckily for me though, Bobby Gould heard about my availibility when he met some of the Leeds coaching-staff while on tour in France, and he decided to give me a chance.

Bobby was the manager at Bristol Rovers at the time and he decided to give me three months to prove myself. It was a chance I had to take or I would have been out of the game.

Those three months were not easy and I had one or two nightmares before eventually signing a contract with the club.

Then it was a matter of learning very quickly in order to survive. A small club like Bristol Rovers can't afford any passengers. It was all very different to life at Leeds.

That was a strange time for Rovers. My first year there was the last at their Eastville ground. After that, we played our home games at Bath City's ground.

The pitch at our new 'home' was terrible. It was always very muddy and bumpy and that didn't make it very easy to play football.

Despite that, I felt my game was improving all the time. Bobby Gould obviously agreed because, soon after becoming Wimbledon's manager in 1987, he came back to sign me.

This was my chance to prove myself in Division One. Wimbledon might not be like most other clubs at this level but I would be facing the best players in the country every week.

Unfortunately, I picked up a few injuries in that first season and that eventually meant I had no chance of making the starting line-up for the FA Cup Final.

I'd played in the semi-final against Luton but soon afterwards picked up a knock. It was touch and go whether I'd even be fit enough to contest a place on the bench.

Thankfully I made it just in time. But I can't remember too much about the day. I haven't even watched the video of the game much since and it all seems a long time ago.

The reason for our success at Wembley was that we played to our strengths. And that means team-work, solid defence and getting the ball in to the opponents' area as quickly as possible.

There was one brief period last season when we seemed to be forgetting those principles and the results went against us. There was a feeling that we were perhaps trying to be too much like a typical Division One side.

So we had a team meeting to sort out a few things. The main factor was making sure that everybody, especially the new signings that Bobby Gould had made, knew exactly what their responsibilities were.

If one Wimbledon player doesn't do his job, everybody else suffers as a result. It's that sort of set-up which has made us such a good away side in the last year or so.

After that meeting we were soon back to the traditional Wimbledon way. People might call it ugly but it works.

Another thing I learnt soon after coming to Plough Lane was that Wimbledon was a club full of businessmen. That doesn't mean just the directors either.

John Fashanu had his clothing business, Alan Cork ran a pub and Lawrie Sanchez a wine-bar. I'm not sure how it happened but somebody must have triggered off the business bug amongst the players.

Well, I wasn't going to be left out of this trend so, with a partner, I opened up a couple of sports shops in my native Yorkshire. We called them 'No Sweat', which is just what it is for me because my partner runs the show most of the time!

I certainly still get enough time to have a few rounds of golf with Alan Cork and some of the other Wimbledon lads. I'm probably the best golfer at the club at the moment so I have to keep my standards high.

But the main business for a Wimbledon player has to be football. I've got another couple of years left on my contract here and I'd certainly like to win at least one more medal during that time.

This time I'd just want to make sure that my contribution is a little longer than 27 minutes.

THE TOWN!

brief for artist JOHN DARGAN.

JOHN DARGAN had two months with Ipswich Town last season — and never kicked a ball. John spent much of his time at Ipswich with the players, but his working gear was not a blue and white strip, but a pair of old overalls.

John's contract at Portman Road was to paint a series of canvasses portraying life with Second Division Ipswich.

He took his place at every home first team and reserve match with sketch pad and camera, to record the action. Then he created a series of oil paintings back at his South London studio.

Millwall fan John was commissioned by Ipswich's main sponsors, Fisons, to produce his paintings, after his earlier scenes at Millwall had been seen by officials at Ipswich Museum.

John graduated with an MA from Chelsea Art College. As a Millwall fan, he asked permission from manager John Docherty to do some paintings at the Den during Millwall's first season in Division One.

His work at Portman Road led to an exhibition at Ipswich Museum.

"I really enjoyed working at Ipswich. Football is a strong visual subject, and I like trying to portray the vitality and life of the game," says John.

ON GUARD

When your immediate opponent is a striker as dangerous and experienced as Coventry's **CYRILLE REGIS**, you need to keep a close watch on him. And that's just what Luton's **DARRON McDONOUGH** is doing here!

TERRY BUTCHER *Rangers*

BRIAN VERSUS BRYAN!

Arsenal's BRIAN MARWOOD battles it out
with BRYAN ROBSON (Manchester United).

CARLTON FAIRWEATHER
Wimbledon

FOR the last few years I've had a very good idea of what I'll be doing when I give up playing football.

When I was still only 20, I was asked to get involved in a soccer school. Once I'd seen how they worked, I got hooked on the idea. I've been involved ever since.

The main idea of the schools is to show boys and girls between the ages of seven and sixteen just how much fun football can be.

I get several of my friends in the game to come along. Amongst those who have helped are my cousins Paul Allen and Clive Allen, Mark Falco, Ossie Ardiles, Jimmy Quinn and Julian Dicks.

I think these schools could really be where my future lies after I hang up my boots. Working with kids really appeals to me.

They've also given me the chance to take a look at the next generation of Allens. Two more of my young cousins have come to the schools in the last couple of years. Both looked at home with a ball at their feet. But when you're a member of the Allen family, people are always making comparisons. Are they better than the others, they ask?

My dad, Dennis Allen, was a professional player himself with Reading in the 60's and my uncle Les, Clive's father, played for Spurs and QPR. Both did well in the game.

It wasn't easy trying to make the grade as a youngster when my cousins were making such a big impact in the game. Clive, one of the country's top goal-scorers, was involved in

LOOK TO THE FUTURE!

several million pound transfers.

Paul burst on to the scene in the 1980 FA Cup Final. At 17 he was the youngest player to play in the final, when he lined up for West Ham against Arsenal.

Meanwhile, I was still at school and could only dream of following my two famous cousins into the game.

At 16, I signed on as an apprentice with QPR, just as Clive returned to the club after a spell with Crystal Palace.

It wasn't easy following Clive to the club where he had made such a name for himself. Everybody expected so much from me and it took time to get used to that pressure.

By the time I made my debut at the age of 19, Clive had moved on again to Tottenham. That meant I could concentrate on establishing myself at Rangers without having people comparing me with him all the time.

Over the next few seasons I established myself as a regular in the midfield. At last, I was more than just the youngest of the Allen cousins.

In any case, there was another Allen coming through at QPR by that stage — Clive's brother, Bradley. He will maintain a great family tradition at Loftus Road. But by then I was beginning to think that it was time to move to another club.

It took a while though to get the move I was looking for. At one stage, I came very close to signing for Arsenal in a joint-move with David Seaman. Unfortunately there was a £200,000 difference in the clubs' valuations and it all fell through. That was a big disappointment, but it made me all the more determined to move on.

Things didn't go well for me

at QPR when Trevor Francis was manager. I got into trouble when, instead of playing a game, I stayed with my wife as she had our first baby. I don't regret that decision. Family life is very important.

For a while it looked as if I wouldn't be allowed to leave. But eventually, after kicking my heels for a long time, I got just the sort of move I was looking for — to West Ham.

BILLY BONDS — inspiring boss

I knew all about life with the Hammers from talking to Paul. There was no doubt it was a bigger club than QPR, even if they were in Division Two.

Lou Macari had signed me for West Ham but after he resigned, Billy Bonds took over as the boss.

There couldn't be a more inspiring boss than Billy. He has always led by example and still beats all of us in the cross-country training runs.

That's just the sort of leadership we needed last season when we'd been dumped out of the Littlewoods Cup semi-finals

by Oldham.

I missed the first leg when the lads lost 6-0 at Oldham but I was back in time for the second game at Upton Park.

Billy Bonds had taken over as boss just before the game and I think we all wanted to get a good result for him. And that's just how it worked out.

That night we won a bit of pride back for ourselves, the club and the fans by winning 3-0. In fact, we gave Oldham a few scares and could have gone very close if the luck had gone our way.

It might not have been enough to take us to Wembley but that result did stir us up in the League.

We'd had to make do without new signings Trevor Morley, Jimmy Quinn and Ian Bishop in the Littlewoods Cup because they were cup-tied. But with them back we had a very strong squad for Billy to choose from.

Unfortunately, we just missed out on a place in the play-offs in the end but we'd shown that there was plenty for the fans to look forward to this season. I don't think we'll be out of the First Division for long.

Billy Bonds has always been a winner and he'll be pulling out all the stops to get us back where we belong.

The boss was just the sort of player that I try to be myself — high fitness level, hard worker, good leadership. Billy had all of those qualities and could play a bit as well.

There's always something to improve on in this game and that's what I aim to do while I'm at West Ham.

The more I learn, the more I will be able to pass on through my soccer schools. I've still got a few years left in the game but all players have to keep an eye on the future. And working with kids is just where I see myself ending up.

That's the advice from West Ham's
MARTIN ALLEN

BRIAN DEANE
Sheffield United

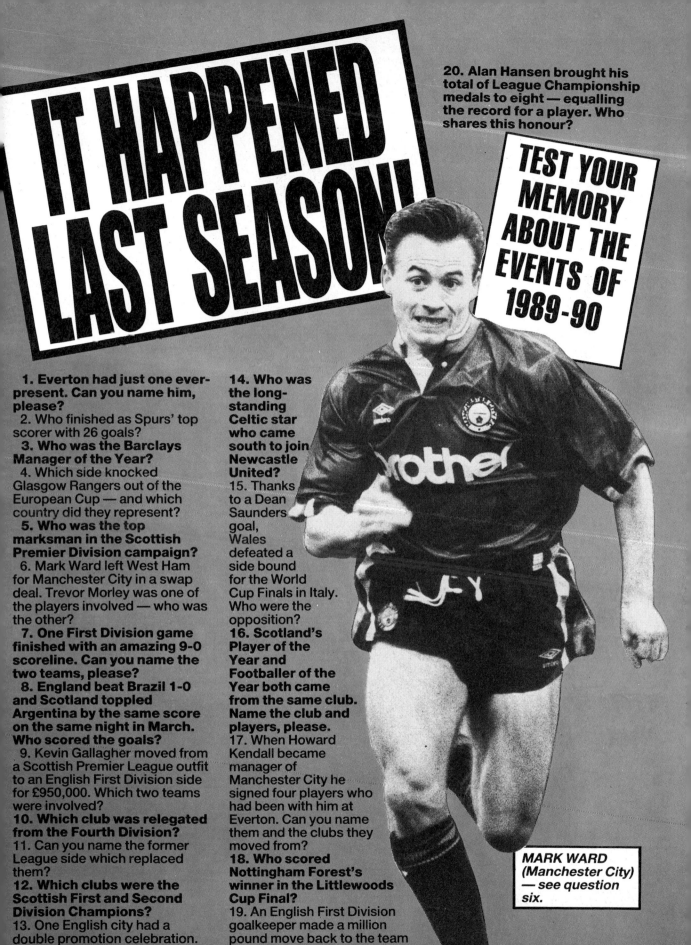

IT HAPPENED LAST SEASON!

20. Alan Hansen brought his total of League Championship medals to eight — equalling the record for a player. Who shares this honour?

TEST YOUR MEMORY ABOUT THE EVENTS OF 1989-90

1. Everton had just one ever-present. Can you name him, please?

2. Who finished as Spurs' top scorer with 26 goals?

3. Who was the Barclays Manager of the Year?

4. Which side knocked Glasgow Rangers out of the European Cup — and which country did they represent?

5. Who was the top marksman in the Scottish Premier Division campaign?

6. Mark Ward left West Ham for Manchester City in a swap deal. Trevor Morley was one of the players involved — who was the other?

7. One First Division game finished with an amazing 9-0 scoreline. Can you name the two teams, please?

8. England beat Brazil 1-0 and Scotland toppled Argentina by the same score on the same night in March. Who scored the goals?

9. Kevin Gallagher moved from a Scottish Premier League outfit to an English First Division side for £950,000. Which two teams were involved?

10. Which club was relegated from the Fourth Division?

11. Can you name the former League side which replaced them?

12. Which clubs were the Scottish First and Second Division Champions?

13. One English city had a double promotion celebration. Name the city and its two teams please.

14. Who was the long-standing Celtic star who came south to join Newcastle United?

15. Thanks to a Dean Saunders goal, Wales defeated a side bound for the World Cup Finals in Italy. Who were the opposition?

16. Scotland's Player of the Year and Footballer of the Year both came from the same club. Name the club and players, please.

17. When Howard Kendall became manager of Manchester City he signed four players who had been with him at Everton. Can you name them and the clubs they moved from?

18. Who scored Nottingham Forest's winner in the Littlewoods Cup Final?

19. An English First Division goalkeeper made a million pound move back to the team he left in 1983. Name the player and the clubs involved please.

> **MARK WARD (Manchester City)** — see question six.

ANSWERS on page 122.

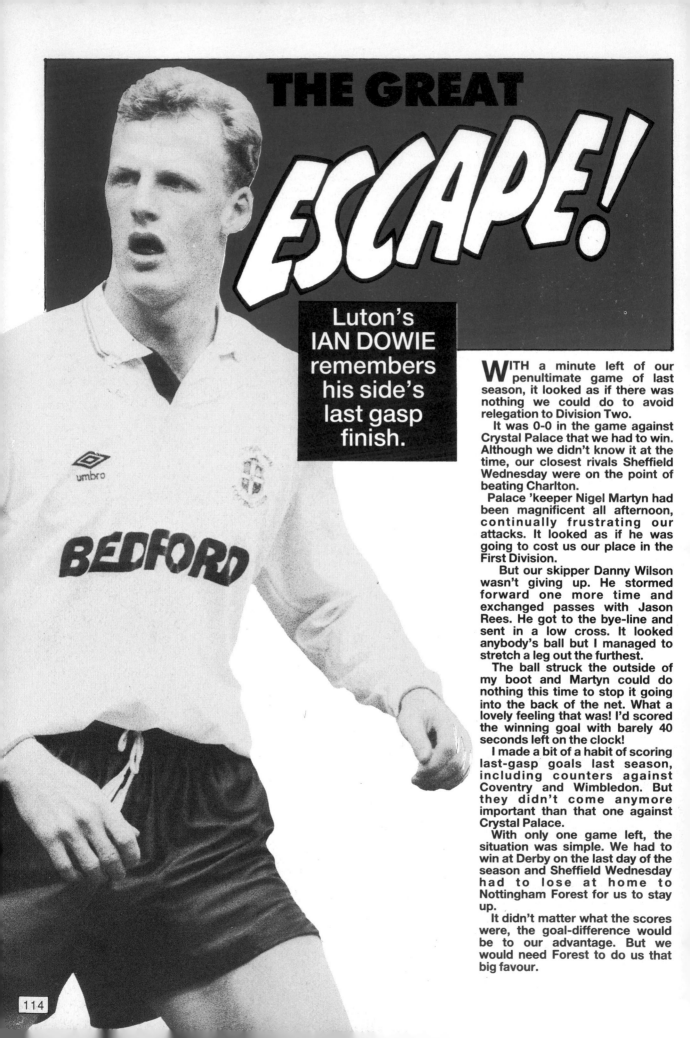

THE GREAT ESCAPE!

Luton's IAN DOWIE remembers his side's last gasp finish.

WITH a minute left of our penultimate game of last season, it looked as if there was nothing we could do to avoid relegation to Division Two.

It was 0-0 in the game against Crystal Palace that we had to win. Although we didn't know it at the time, our closest rivals Sheffield Wednesday were on the point of beating Charlton.

Palace 'keeper Nigel Martyn had been magnificent all afternoon, continually frustrating our attacks. It looked as if he was going to cost us our place in the First Division.

But our skipper Danny Wilson wasn't giving up. He stormed forward one more time and exchanged passes with Jason Rees. He got to the bye-line and sent in a low cross. It looked anybody's ball but I managed to stretch a leg out the furthest.

The ball struck the outside of my boot and Martyn could do nothing this time to stop it going into the back of the net. What a lovely feeling that was! I'd scored the winning goal with barely 40 seconds left on the clock!

I made a bit of a habit of scoring last-gasp goals last season, including counters against Coventry and Wimbledon. But they didn't come anymore important than that one against Crystal Palace.

With only one game left, the situation was simple. We had to win at Derby on the last day of the season and Sheffield Wednesday had to lose at home to Nottingham Forest for us to stay up.

It didn't matter what the scores were, the goal-difference would be to our advantage. But we would need Forest to do us that big favour.

To be honest, I was more worried about that than our ability to beat Derby. After all, we had much more to play for than our opponents.

But Forest gave us a clue that they would cause Wednesday problems when they won the Littlewoods Cup Final against Oldham. After that, they were full of confidence and beat Manchester United 4-0 in a League game.

When that last Saturday came, we just had to concentrate on our own game and hope that Forest could produce something special.

GREAT START

THE crucial day couldn't have started any better. After just 66 seconds, right-back Tim Breacker hit a 25-yard screamer past Peter Shilton to put us 1-0 up.

Tim doesn't score too many goals but that was quite a time to pull one out — especially against a 'keeper of Shilton's quality.

That gave us all the confidence we needed and in the 19th minute we went 2-0 up when Kingsley Black scored. Surely we could win the match from this position!

But, perhaps understandably, we sat back on our lead. And that was to prove very costly. Mark Wright got Derby back in to the game in the 29th minute, and then in injury-time of the first half they equalised.

We'd thrown all our hard work away but there was, at least, some good news waiting for us in the dressing-room at half-time. Nottingham Forest were 1-0 up on Sheffield Wednesday.

We knew then that there was plenty to play for in the second-half. But we still had to get a third goal from somewhere.

It came in the 75th minute — again from Kingsley Black. Not the prettiest of goals — the ball bobbled along the ground and went in off the post — but nobody cared about that.

After that we did everything we could to keep possession and stop Derby from scoring again. And with just a few minutes to go I heard the news we'd all been waiting for.

Mark Wright went down injured and while there was a break in play a message came that Forest were now 3-0 up.

That news soon filtered through the crowd and they cheered us all the way to the final whistle.

I did feel sorry for Wednesday. They're a great club who deserve to be in Division One. But I knew we'd done enough ourselves to be worth our place. It wasn't just

a freak of the results as far as we were concerned.

We'd not had a lot of luck all season. Decisions had gone against us at vital times, important players had been injured and others had been sold.

First Division survival was very important both to the club and the players. We've got a lot of youngsters in the side and I'm not too sure how they would have survived in the much more physical Division Two.

From my point of view, I was very glad to have another chance of playing at the highest level. It would have been very disappointing to be relegated after my first full season in Division One.

Luton had signed me the year before from non-League Hendon. That was quite a jump to make from the Vauxhall-Opel League to the First Division.

I had a good job with British Aerospace, having taken a Masters degree in Mechanical Engineering at Hatfield Polytechnic. So money certainly wasn't a major consideration in my decision.

But despite having a good job, there was no way I was going to pass-up the chance of becoming a professional footballer.

Ironically, I made my full debut for Luton in a Littlewoods Cup quarter-final against Southampton, the club who had ruined my dreams as a schoolboy.

Although I'm six feet tall now, Southampton had let me go because I was too small. I was a late-developer and they didn't see the best of me at the Dell. After I left there I played for a number of non-League outfits while doing my five-year course at college.

The last of those clubs was Hendon, where the goals really started to go in. During the season before Luton signed me I scored 35 goals in 30 games, not bad at any level.

When I joined Luton, it obviously meant giving up my job at British Aerospace. But I always try to keep up with developments in the field so I'll be ready to go back when my football career is over.

I realised straight away that I still had a lot to learn about football. Going to a Division One club in the middle of the season wasn't very easy. What I needed was the benefit

of pre-season training. It wasn't a lack of fitness that was the problem, more a case of doing some more work with the ball.

It was going to take some time but I would have plenty of help along the way. As well as the coaching staff at Luton, I had my dad to tell me what I was doing wrong.

He played professional football for Bangor in Northern Ireland before he had to retire with an ankle injury. So he knows what he's talking about.

Dad comes to every game and he's both my biggest fan and harshest critic. If I'm doing something wrong, he'll help me to put it right.

I soon found I had something else to thank my dad for as well. That came when Billy Bingham called me up for the Northern Ireland squad.

Although I was born in England, both my parents came from Belfast and I certainly think of myself as being Irish.

International football is a great bonus for me. When I was working for British Aerospace, playing League football was just a dream. To have represented my country as well is a great honour.

But there's still no doubt in my mind — that win at Derby is the best thing that's happened in my career so far. Without that escape-act I wouldn't still be playing First Division football and nothing beats that.

DANNY WILSON

Non-stop HIGHBURY

Why Arsenal's H.Q. is a hive of round-the-clock action.

THE ARSENAL — once it was the most famous name in football. The club dominated English football throughout the 1930's, and established a world-wide reputation.

In modern times, the Arsenal name has been overtaken by Manchester United and Liverpool as a symbol of the 'best of English', although the Gunners did fight back by winning the First Division Championship in 1989.

But off the field, Arsenal still lead the way. In terms of their involvement with the local community, Arsenal are 'way out in front.

Last year they completed a new £1.5 million Sports Centre attached to Highbury Stadium. This is in so much demand by the fans the players rarely get to use it!

"We built our Sports Centre with the community and our supporters in mind," says Arsenal chairman Peter Hill-Wood.

"We know of few other institutions which make this sort of commitment to the local community. We wish the best of luck to the Islington Education Service in their endeavours to provide the best educational opportunities for local people.

"For more than 50 years Arsenal Football Club has enjoyed a special relationship with Islington Schools. We provide kit, footballs, and training time at our indoor centre, plus financial donations and the use of the stadium for special matches."

It's not only school children who benefit from the facilities at Highbury. A full range of sporting activities are available for adults.

There are indoor cricket and football leagues; indoor tennis coaching; carpet bowls; indoor hockey; plus a full range of weight-training, keep-fit and aerobics sessions.

Peter Hill-Wood — Arsenal chairman.

The main hall at the Sports Centre is in use for 16 hours a day. Even if Arsenal manager George Graham wanted his players to train indoors on the Astro-turf surface, he'd have a job finding a free slot in the schedule.

The facilities are available for any member of the local community, or Arsenal supporter. Not forgetting all the local schools.

The senior men's five-a-side football championship attracted an entry this year of 112 teams, and there were separate competitions for Under-16's, Under-12's and an Over-35's veteran division.

Arsenal also stage ladies' football, and run two women's football teams in local leagues.

For three years the Gunners have had girl football trainees on the staff at Highbury. This year there are nine girls

They train at Highbury, and play for the ladies' teams, while helping out with coaching and training sessions at schools.

The girls promote football in local schools, while studying Leisure and Recreation courses at college.

Arsenal also have a squad of top young tennis trainees. They were recruited from around the country, and live in digs close to Highbury. They train and practise under the eagle eye of a professional coach every morning from eight o'clock. Now there are three hockey trainees — two boys and a girl — on the Highbury books.

Each week there are two bowls sessions. They last for two hours and cost only 50p a time — with

tea and biscuits included.

Indoor cricket is played on Monday and Friday evenings. Tennis on Sunday afternoon and evening. Hockey on Thursday afternoons.

The rest of the week the sports hall is in constant use for five or seven-a-side football leagues or training sessions. While the smaller hall is almost as busy with weight-training sessions for men and women every evening, and most lunch-times, plus aerobics classes several days a week.

At the same time, the Arsenal 'Action Sport' staff also organise

charity fund-raising events like a Swimathon, or fun-runs. The National Children's Home, based in the Highbury area, was Arsenal's 'designated' charity this year.

During the school holidays, Arsenal stage 'soccer schools' for children, to give them somewhere to go during the day.

The Sports Centre at Highbury

used to consist of only an indoor training area for the players. But it has been completely re-built as part of the new 'Clock end' development of the main ground.

It now includes a restaurant, conference facilities, and executive boxes. Supporters can enjoy special pre-match hospitality with a champagne reception, three-course meal, cabaret and video show.

But that is for the well-to-do fan. The club has kept the Sports Centre very much a place for the average local supporter, with prices kept to a minimum.

"We will always remember that the most important people are the fans who turn up every week," says Peter Hill-Wood. "We want them to bring their children, who will become the next generation of Arsenal supporters.

"Arsenal are delighted to be playing our part in the activities of the local community. We believe this is a vital role for the club."

DES
TO WEAR

WHEN Stuart McCall started his football career he had two major ambitions. One was to sample First Division football — the other was to play for Scotland. He's achieved both these aims — but not without a struggle!

Stuart made his professional debut with Bradford City in 1982. At the time it seemed that both Stuart's ambitions were a long way off as the Valley Parade outfit were in the Third Division at the time.

But soon Stuart was attracting the attention of international selectors. In November 1984, both England and Scotland laid claim to the youngster by selecting him for Under-21 duty.

McCall was born in Leeds, but since he had a Scottish father, he was eligible for both countries.

"I literally had 30 minutes to make up my mind," he explains. "It was a difficult decision for a 20-year-old to make.

"In the end I listened to the advice of City's management team at the time, Trevor Cherry and Terry Yorath.

"They told me to choose England and I did. But even as the squad assembled for an away game in Turkey, my heart just wasn't in it.

"I was named as one of the substitutes. In the last minute manager Dave Sexton told me to warm up. He aimed to put me on the park to give me a cap.

"I knew that if this happened, I would be disqualified from playing for Scotland.

"Right or wrong, I felt it was simply an insurance policy on England's part. That they wanted me capped just to make sure no one else could pick me.

"So with only seconds to go, I fiddled about with my tie-ups,

PERATE
DARK BLUE!
That was Everton's STUART McCALL

hoping to delay the substitution. Then the referee blew his whistle for time up. I was very relieved not to have played.

"As soon as I returned to Bradford I told Trevor I couldn't let myself be called up again by England.

"I didn't know if I'd wrecked my Scotland prospects by refusing their original approach. But even if I never played international football again, I just had to reveal how I felt.

"I received two England shirts after the Turkish game. I gave one to City team-mate Greg Abbott and kept the other.

"Eventually I put mine up for auction to raise funds for the Bradford fire victims. I'm glad it went to a good cause.

"The only problem was replacing it with a Scotland jersey. I wanted a dark blue jersey so badly that my wife actually bought me one for a Christmas present one year."

Then Stuart's hopes of getting that elusive Scotland jersey were enhanced when he moved from Second Division Bradford to top flight Everton.

But Stuart himself doesn't believe that playing for Bradford really hindered his international prospects.

"I don't believe my cap chances would have suffered had I stayed with City," he claims. "After all, I was first called up to an Under-21 squad when we were in the Third Division, and we were still in the Second when I was drafted in to the Scotland squad for the full international against Spain in 1988. I didn't play, but it was useful experience.

"Unfortunately, being a City player might have cost me my first cap.

"I had been selected for a 'B'

international against France at Pittodrie in April 1987. But I had to call off because City had a re-arranged League match that midweek. Ian Wilson — then with Leicester City, but who later became a team-mate at Goodison — was called in to take my place.

"He played against the French and went on to win five caps before I'd even got one!"

But if a player is to win international recognition, playing for a top team in big competitions is the way to catch the eye.

It certainly did Stuart no harm to make a Wembley Cup Final appearance in 1989. And although he ended on the losing side, his two goals — his second being rated one of the finest ever seen at Wembley — certainly helped to bring his name to the fore.

"Those goals at Wembley gave me a great boost," Stuart admits. "I would have been looking forward to last season in any case after having got my settling-in period out of the way, but I couldn't wait for it to start after that.

"Again, our League form was a bit up and down, although we led the First Division at one time.

"That was when I was recalled to the Scotland squad and Steve Clarke, of Chelsea — who were also near the top at that time — was also brought back in.

"I'm not saying that the only reason we were re-introduced was because our clubs were doing well. But the spotlight will also be on you when that happens."

One factor which helped Stuart find his best form was playing with Norman Whiteside.

"Norman and I take it in turns to go forward," explains Stuart. "As a result, I'm getting into the box more often, and that's pleased me

NORMAN WHITESIDE

a lot."

It was that form which saw him win his first full cap against Argentina last season and go on to gain a place in Scotland's World Cup squad. Stuart had succeeded in his second objective — that dark blue jersey was his at last.

WHAT A SEASON!

HOW OLDHAM ATHLETIC HIT THE HEADLINES — AGAIN AND AGAIN!

A LITTLEWOODS Cup Final, two FA Cup semi-finals and a promotion battle that went right up the 46th and final League game of the campaign. That was the action-packed programme for Oldham Athletic last season.

Nobody expected anything like that from Joe Royle's men at the start of last term. But by the end of May, the likes of Mike Milligan, Rick Holden and Andy Ritchie were household names. This is a blow-by-blow account of how the battlers from Boundary Park made the headlines.

AUGUST 19:
Oldham kick-off the League campaign away from home with a single goal defeat from Lancashire rivals Blackburn Rovers.

AUGUST 26:
A 2-2 scoreline at home to Swindon disappoints Joe Royle, as does an injury sustained by key centre-half Andy Holden.

AUGUST 31:
The draw for the second round of the Littlewoods Cup is made. Oldham have a tough two-legged tie against Division Two promotion favourites Leeds United. An early cup knock-out seems on the cards.

SEPTEMBER 19:
Leeds visit Boundary Park for the first-leg of the Littlewoods Cup game. A tight return match is expected as Oldham win 2-1.

OCTOBER 3:
Another 2-1 win against Leeds at Elland Road, sees Oldham through to round three of the Littlewoods Cup. They are drawn at home to Division Four giant-killers Scarborough, conquerors of First Division Chelsea.

OCTOBER 21:
A 2-0 home win against Middlesbrough keeps Latics in mid-table. But all eyes are on Wednesday night, and the Scarborough game.

OCTOBER 25:
7-0! A memorable night for all concerned but especially Frankie Bunn. The Oldham striker hammers home six goals as the Seasiders are well and truly sunk. The televised fourth round draw pairs Latics with League champions Arsenal. A sell-out Boundary Park is a certainty.

NOVEMBER 22:
Night of the big game and Oldham are all fired up. They enter this game on the back of an eight-match unbeaten run which has taken them up the Second Division table into sixth place. Arsenal top the First but this counts for nothing as they are sent back to North London 3-1 losers. Nick Henry bags a rare goal but Andy Ritchie is the hero with a double strike.

JOE ROYLE

EARL BARRETT

RICK HOLDEN

IAN MARSHALL

MIKE MILLIGAN

DECEMBER 1:

The unbeaten run has been stretched to ten games, but Friday night visitors Blackburn are the severest test yet. But Oldham come through 2-0 winners, and so jump above Rovers into fifth spot.

DECEMBER 9:

Drawn to travel to Southampton for a Littlewoods Cup quarter-final date, the players tune in to see who they will meet in the FA Cup third round. It's Birmingham City away.

DECEMBER 16:

Oldham keep up the pressure on League leaders Leeds and Sheffield United. Today's 2-0 win at West Ham is followed by a Boxing Day win over Port Vale and draws at home to Portsmouth and, more significantly, away to Leeds.

JANUARY 6:

Mixed fortunes for Frankie Bunn. His goal earns the side an FA Cup replay date with Birmingham, but he badly injures a knee. No date is set for his return to fitness.

JANUARY 10:

Joe Royle may have a talented squad, but it isn't a big one. Frankie Bunn's injury tempts Joe into the transfer market. Neil Redfearn joins from Watford for £150,000. That night Neil watches his new team-mates in action against Birmingham. Even without Bunn plus striking partner and injury victim Andy Ritchie, they progress to round four of the FA Cup. Brighton will visit Boundary Park for that.

JANUARY 20:

A 1-1 home draw with promotion rivals Newcastle keeps Oldham in fourth place in Division Two.

JANUARY 24:

For their Littlewoods Cup quarter-final, the players and officials fly to Southampton. This is to avoid a tiring road journey. It's a great success as an Andy Ritchie equaliser in injury time earns the team a Boundary Park replay.

JANUARY 27:

More Cup joy. This time it's the FA Cup and Brighton are the 2-1 losers. Athletic go on to meet mighty Everton in the fifth round.

JANUARY 31:

Oldham's ninth cup game of the campaign sees Southampton knocked out of the Littlewoods Cup. Andy Ritchie and Mike Milligan are the goal heroes in a 2-0 victory.

FEBRUARY 14:

The club's first-ever Littlewoods Cup semi-final, and West Ham United travel north to contest the first leg. Oldham go goal crazy and end up 6-0 winners. The second leg looks a formality and the club's commercial manager, Alan Hardy, even orders £30,000 worth of Littlewoods Cup Final souvenirs.

FEBRUARY 17:

Another big cup match and a Boundary Park lock-out. Everton are the visitors for the FA Cup fifth round tie. When they take a two-goal lead through Graeme Sharp and Tony Cottee it looks all over for Oldham. But an Andy Ritchie penalty and Roger Palmer's fourth goal in as many games means a Goodison Park replay.

FEBRUARY 21:

A scorching match at Everton finishes level again and so it's back to Oldham to see who will meet Division One title-chasers Aston Villa in the quarter-finals.

MARCH 7:

The second-leg of the Littlewoods Cup semi-final sees Latics go down 3-0 to West Ham. Manager Joe Royle isn't happy, he said it takes the gloss off that 6-0 first leg win. But 3000 travelling fans don't mind. They're going to Wembley for the first time ever with Oldham.
Meanwhile, crackshot Andy Ritchie misses the game with knee trouble. It looks as though he'll be out of action for some time.

MARCH 10:

Everton are back at Boundary Park for the second replay of the FA Cup fifth round tie. It goes to extra-time before an Ian Marshall penalty clinches it for Oldham! It's a doubly successful day for Joe Royle. He's selected as manager of the month for February.

MARCH 14:

Aston Villa next — no problem. The Latics breeze past Graham Taylor's high fliers 3-0. Now they're on course for their second semi-final of the season, this time against local rivals Manchester United.

MARCH 17:

League action brings a 1-0 defeat at relegation-haunted Barnsley. It looks as though Oldham's cup exploits could be taking toll.

MARCH 21:

With the transfer deadline rapidly approaching, Joe Royle splashes out a club record £225,000 for Bournemouth's former Manchester City scoring ace Paul Moulden.

APRIL 8:

Maine Road, Manchester. The venue for the FA Cup semi-final between Athletic and Manchester United. It's Oldham's 53rd game of the season and, without doubt, one of the most important. Earl Barrett gives Oldham an early lead before the First Division giants roar back to go ahead through England men Webb and Robson. Ian Marshall equalises before Danny Wallace and then Roger Palmer make it three all after extra-time and on to a replay.

APRIL 11:

Heartache. Manchester United "super-sub" Mark Robins scores the extra-time goal that ends Oldham's double Wembley dream. They go down 2-1.

APRIL 13:

Leeds United must be sick of the sight of Oldham as they brush the League leaders aside 3-1 at Boundary Park. All through the season, manager Joe Royle has insisted promotion is the priority. With games in hand over the other play-off clubs it's looking good.

APRIL 24:

CRASH! A 2-1 reverse at Portsmouth makes three defeats out of four games for Oldham. But this loss is worsened further with Earl Barrett suffering concussion. There are fears he won't be fit for Sunday's Littlewoods Cup Final. That would mean joining the ruled-out Andy Holden on the Wembley sidelines.

APRIL 29:

Wembley. A glorious sunny day for 75,000 Nottingham Forest and Oldham fans and a perfect pitch for the players. Andy Ritchie and Frankie Bunn have both come through the last four or five games and so are ready to play the full ninety minutes, while Earl Barrett is also declared fit for his big day. But Oldham lose 1-0 to a Nigel Jemson strike. It still rates as a memorable day in the club's history.

MAY 1:

Oxford United at home is the first of four matches Oldham must win to assure themselves of a place in the play-offs. Recent poor League form, possibly because the players' minds were wandering towards Wembley, has affected their promotion chances. A Rick Holden hat-trick sends them on their way to a 4-1 win. Now for Wolves in two days.

MAY 3:

Football can be so cruel. A Wolves equaliser in the last minute means Oldham must rely on other teams slipping up on the final Saturday of the season. Final score in this one is 1-1.

MAY 5:

Oldham pull out all the stops to win 3-2 at Sunderland who are already assured of their play-off berth. But Blackburn get the point they need at home to Brighton and Oldham have missed out on the promotion play-offs. They are appreciated, though, by the Roker Park fans. They cheer the visitors off.

MAY 7:

Oldham play their final game of the season away to Bradford. It is the 64th of the season and they have won nothing but a lot of friends. Manager Joe Royle is heavily tipped to become Manager of the Year, but the award instead goes to Kenny Dalglish. Joe and his players must make do with tired legs, and a lot of memories from an amazing season.

CONGRATULATIONS! IT'S A RECORD!! THE HUNDREDTH TIME YOU'VE BEEN SENT OFF!

MIRROR, MIRROR, ON THE WALL — WHO IS THE FAIREST OF THEM ALL?

REFEREES ONLY.

THAT'S A GOOD START. GETTING SENT OFF FOR FIGHTING OVER WHO WON THE TOSS!

ON THE FUNNY SIDE!

LOOK! I KNOW IT'S THE FIRST CLUB YOU'VE EVER MANAGED — BUT IT'S THE PLAYERS WHO EXCHANGE SHIRTS!

HOME MANAGER   VISITOR MANAGER

YOU'LL NEVER WALK ALONE!!

HE ONLY ASKED IF YOU'D ENJOYED THE MATCH!!!

AND YOUR DAD — HE'S WELL?

ANSWERS TO IT HAPPENED LAST SEASON (ON P113)

1. Neville Southall.
2. Gary Lineker.
3. Kenny Dalglish (Liverpool).
4. Bayern Munich of West Germany.
5. John Robertson (Hearts).
6. Ian Bishop.
7. Liverpool were the victors over Crystal Palace.
8. Gary Lineker and Stewart McKimmie.
9. Dundee United transferred the player to Coventry City.
10. Colchester United.
11. Darlington.
12. St Johnstone and Brechin City respectively.
13. Bristol Rovers (Division Three Champions: Bristol City (runners-up).
14. Roy Aitken.
15. Costa Rica.
16. Aberdeen's Jim Bett was Players' Player and Alex
McLeish was Footballer of the Year
17. Wayne Clarke from Leicester; Alan Harper from Sheffield Wednesday; Peter Reid from Queen's Park Rangers and Adrian Heath from Aston Villa.
18. Nigel Jemson.
19. John Lukic moved from Arsenal to Leeds.
20. Phil Neal.

WE'VE WEATHERED THE STORM!

LAST season was a period of change at Parkhead and it showed in what was a disappointing time as far as results went! But I'm sure we've weathered the worst of the storm.

Roy Aitken and Tommy Burns moved on within a month of each other, which left a large gap to fill. Between them they had spent 30 years with Celtic. Their departure left us a bit short on experience.

Now only myself, Paul McStay and Peter Grant are left of the players who started as schoolboys at Parkhead.

It was strange for a time when Roy and Tommy left. They had been part of my day-to-day life ever since I joined the ground staff, right through my time in the reserves and then in the first team.

Their experience on the park and in the dressing-room had been very important. Hopefully we are the players who can take over their role.

That's why I thought the appointment of Paul McStay as captain was so important. There was simply no one else for the job. He's a Celtic man through and through and always has been.

Certainly he's a different kind of leader from Roy. For one thing he's far quieter, although who isn't? He tends to lead more by example and being such a gifted player his performances can lift the whole team.

Naturally he has started to shout a bit more and it probably won't be long before

Celtic's DEREK WHYTE looks ahead.

he's rivalling Roy's level!

It was all the more satisfying to see Paul take over since we both joined Celtic as schoolboys.

Celtic have always put a lot of emphasis on their youth policy and I hope that doesn't change. Some clubs rely mainly on big money signings, but I've always believed a team should be allowed to grow. You can't rely only on buying in talent.

Celtic's good youth policy was a deciding factor in my signing as a 13-year-old. If I was a young boy now signing for a big club I'd be wondering whether I'd ever be given the chance to break through.

Thankfully for me, and many others, Celtic are willing to do so.

Don't get me wrong. I'm not against a club signing players from outside. No team can survive on home grown talent alone. And neither do I believe that players coming from other clubs are less committed.

Paul Elliott is the perfect example. After a shaky start we've built a good understanding in the centre of defence.

When Paul arrived a lot of the Press immediately wrote him off. He didn't let it get to him though and everyone knows how well he performed once he settled down.

Paul was unlucky to pick up an injury early on and then he had an illness which put him on the sidelines for a long spell.

He came back very strongly from that and really shone in the big games last term.

I just hope some of Paul's determination has rubbed off on me. Although I missed out on the Scotland squad to Italy I'm sure I can work my way back in.

Andy Roxburgh has such a number of quality central defenders to choose from it won't be easy, but at 22 I've got time on my side.

It was disappointing not to be chosen for the squad for the finals although like the rest of the Celtic side I wasn't playing at my best last term.

At least being picked for the two B internationals showed me I was still in the manager's thoughts. Now it's up to me to prove I'm good enough to play again for my country.

My priorities still lie at Parkhead though. I want to see us back in contention in the League before I have any thoughts of returning to the international scene.

Like everyone who plays for Celtic I give 100% on the park and at training but when I'm away from Parkhead I try to forget all about it.

With the amount of coverage given to the Old Firm in Glasgow it's a relief to escape it. Whatever job you do you don't want to spend all your time thinking about it.

Team-mate Andy Walker's father introduced me to a Glasgow tennis club last year and it's been a great move. I've played for a number of years when away on holiday but now I can get a more regular game.

I know a lot of footballers like to play golf, but to me it's not physical enough, whereas tennis is.

The only other hobby I have is sleeping! I've always been able to nod off in the afternoon for an hour or two, even when we were going through the rough patch last season.

Hopefully this season will see me fulfilling some of the dreams I've had.

Paul McStay

YOUR PICTURE GUIDE!
ACTION! PIN-UPS! COLOUR!

Printed and Published in Great Britain by D. C. THOMSON & CO., LTD., 185 Fleet Street, London EC4A 2HS.
© D. C. THOMSON & CO., LTD., 1990.
ISBN 0 85116 492 7

DALE GORDON (NORWICH)

All sorts of players from a variety of teams — but they all know how to celebrate a goal!

PAT BONNER (CELTIC)

IAN BRIGHTWELL (MANCHESTER CITY)